575
MGA
1st

# The Best of British Architecture
## 1980 to 2000

Noel Moffett

A. and N. Moffett
Architects and Planning Consultants

**E & FN SPON**
An Imprint of Chapman & Hall
London · Glasgow · New York · Tokyo · Melbourne · Madras

**Published by E & FN Spon, an imprint of Chapman & Hall, 2–6 Boundary Row, London SE1 8HN**

Chapman & Hall, 2–6 Boundary Row, London SE1 8HN, UK

Blackie Academic & Professional, Wester Cleddens Road, Bishopbriggs, Glasgow G64 2NZ, UK

Chapman & Hall Inc., 29 West 35th Street, New York NY10001, USA

Chapman & Hall Japan, Thomson Publishing Japan, Hirakawacho Nemoto Building, 6F, 1-7-11 Hirakawa-cho, Chiyoda-ku, Tokyo 102, Japan

Chapman & Hall Australia, Thomas Nelson Australia, 102 Dodds Street, South Melbourne, Victoria 3205, Australia

Chapman & Hall India, R. Seshadri, 32 Second Main Road, CIT East, Madras 600 035, India

First edition 1993

© 1993 Noel Moffett

Designed by Maximus Associates, Friern Barnet, London

Typeset in Univers by Photoprint, Torquay, Devon

Printed in Great Britain by Warwick Printing Company Limited, Warwick

ISBN 0 419 17240 8

A catalogue record for this book is available from the British Library

Library of Congress Cataloging-in-Publication data available

Front cover: The Ark Office Building, Hammersmith, West London – Ralph Erskine with Lennart Bergstrom and Rock Townsend.

Back cover: (clockwise from top left) Hong Kong and Shanghai Bank – Sir Norman Foster; Design for Office Building in Berlin – Zaha Hadid; Hostel for the Physically Handicapped, Hampshire, UK – Colin Stansfield Smith; The Lloyds Building, London – Sir Richard Rogers.

# CONTENTS

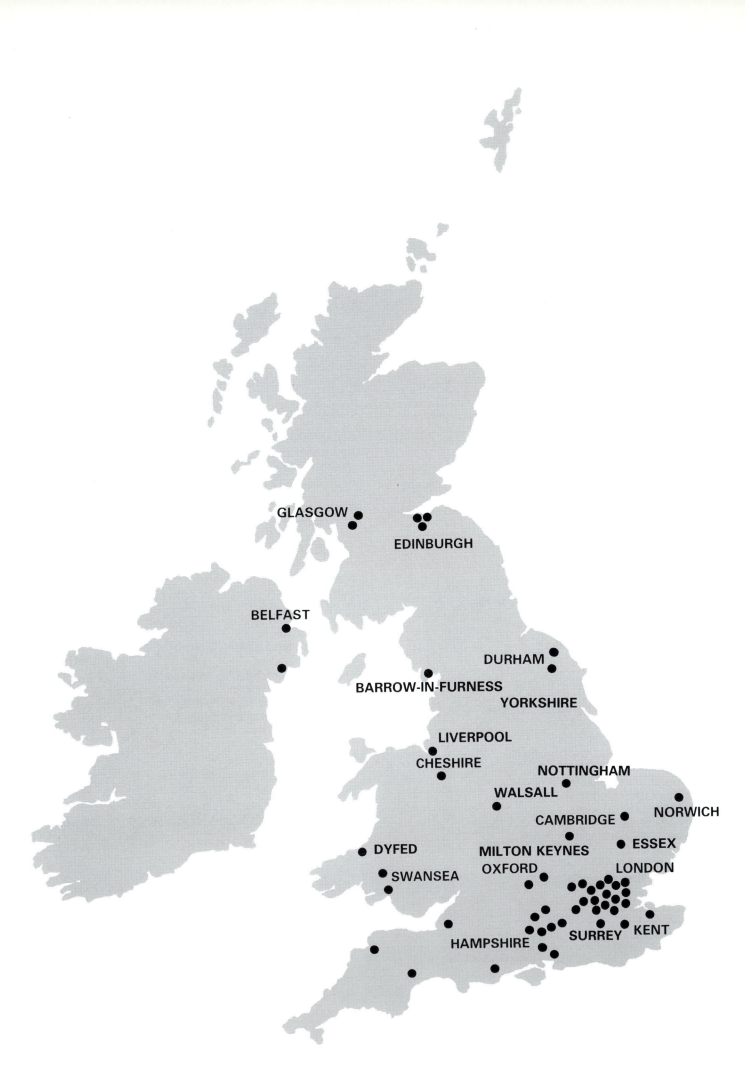

GLASGOW

EDINBURGH

BELFAST

DURHAM

BARROW-IN-FURNESS

YORKSHIRE

LIVERPOOL

CHESHIRE

NOTTINGHAM

WALSALL

CAMBRIDGE

NORWICH

DYFED

MILTON KEYNES

ESSEX

SWANSEA

OXFORD

LONDON

HAMPSHIRE

SURREY

KENT

Location of buildings and projects in the United Kingdom.

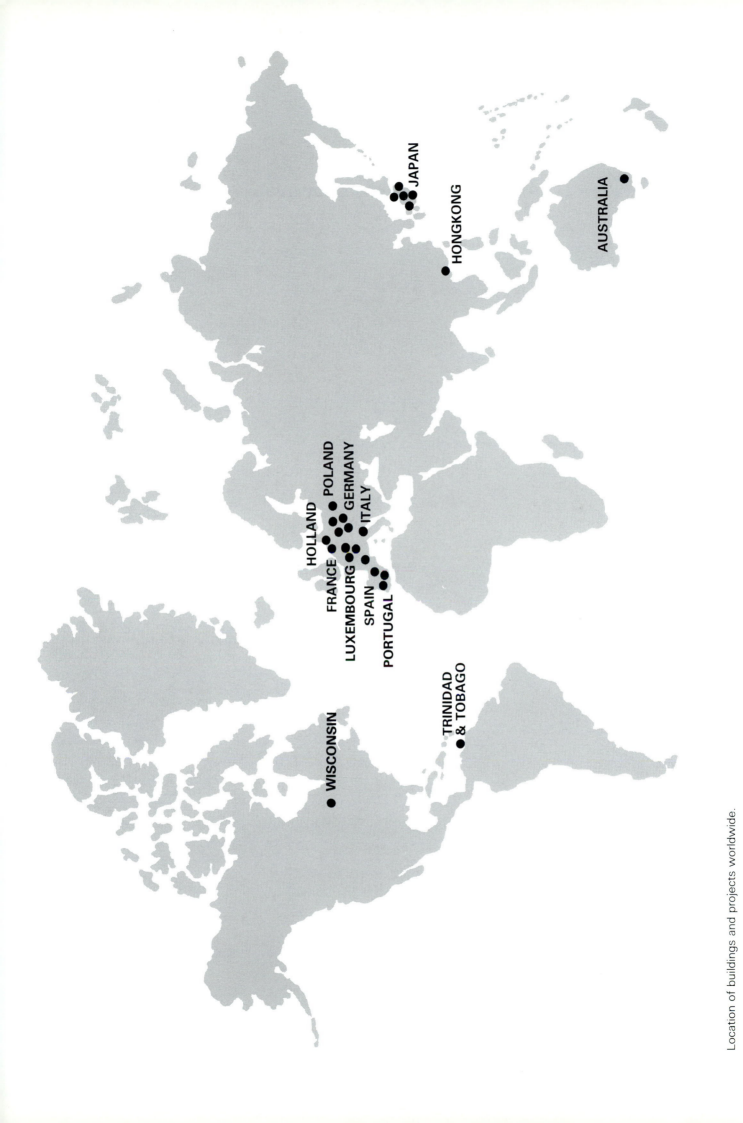

Location of buildings and projects worldwide.

**For ALINA**
*constructive critic, positive consultant and dedicated worker.*

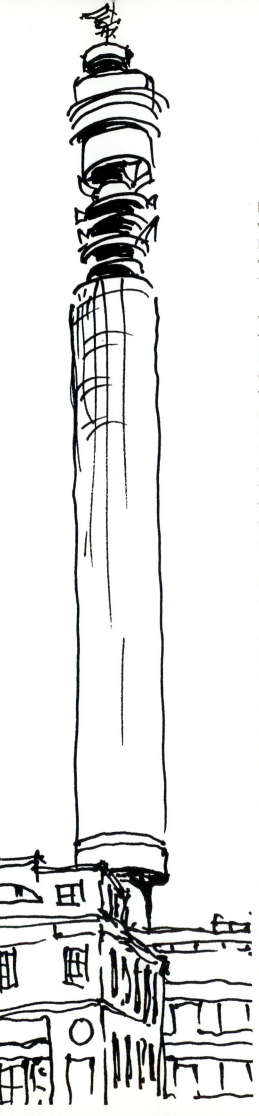

# PREFACE

If we look for one word which would characterize the state of British architecture today it would probably be 'chaotic' or 'eclectic'.

I'm reminded of a bicycle wheel. Someone has removed the tyre and the rim and left a lot of spokes pointing in different directions. There used to be just one direction for architecture: when the Modern Movement began, Gropius, Mies van der Rohe and Le Corbusier showed the way and we all followed. But we didn't take the public with us and that way led to disaster – to the erection of huge bleak housing estates, to glass-and-steel point blocks of offices, to 'the international style' and 'comprehensive redevelopment' – and to extreme unpopularity with the public.

Happily Gaudi, Aalto and Frank Lloyd Wright gradually pushed us in a different direction – a less bleak, more human, more interesting and more acceptable one – and architecture slowly became multi-directional.

This book suggests that British architecture, as the new century approaches, is moving in ten different directions. Each chapter examines one of these directions and gives examples of some of the significant buildings which our architects have designed in that category – at home and overseas.

The book in fact is perhaps the first comprehensive critical survey of the best of end-of-the-century British architecture. It should be of interest to students of architecture throughout the world – perplexed by the multi-directional way in which today's architecture is developing – and to all those interested in the quality of our environment. It is also perhaps an answer to the Prince of Wales' harsh words about 'modern' architecture, illustrating and commenting on, as it does, buildings which he dislikes as well as a few of his favourites.

At first glance it may seem that the chapter headings in this book refer to the so-called 'styles' of architecture. This is not so. Rather they refer to the architect's attitude to the design of his or her building and the way in which that attitude is expressed. 'Hi-Tech' is not a style, it is a way of designing and building; 'Participation' demonstrates the close collaboration between client, architect and the people for whom the building is being designed; 'Fun' embodies the way in which the building itself gives pleasure, enjoyment – and occasionally excitement – to the user.

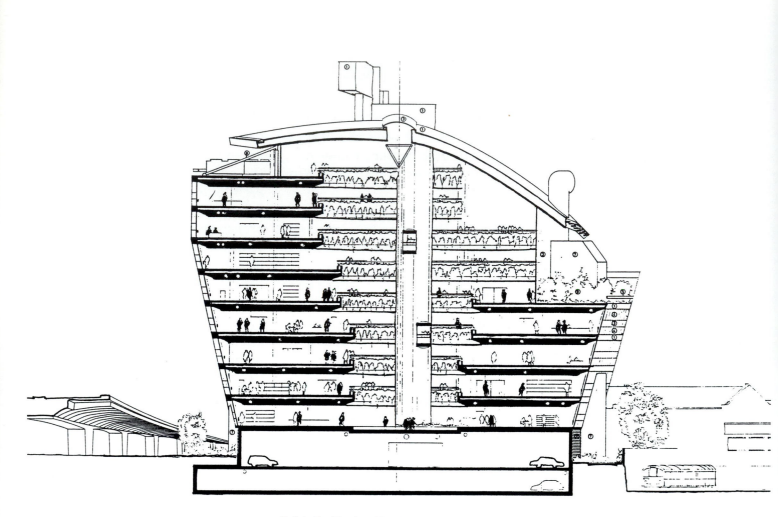

Ralph Erskine's office building in London

# FOREWORD by Dennis Sharp

British architecture of the past decade has been much admired throughout the world. After a long period in the doldrums and notwithstanding all the difficulties there have been in getting 'good' buildings through the quagmires of local authority and national planning requirements, a number of high peaks in architectural design have been reached. British architecture has been widely reported and featured in books and international journals. Many foreign competition prizes and commissions have been awarded to successful British practices.

Three names in particular have dominated this period and the international scene: Sir Richard Rogers, Sir Norman Foster and Sir James Stirling. Their work has been the subject of many books and critical studies. They have produced buildings in various parts of the world and they have fuelled discussion and controversy over architectural issues. Few lay people would claim to be ignorant of the Lloyds Building in London or the new terminal at London's Stansted Airport or indeed the colourful *Staatsgalerie* in Stuttgart. However, this contribution to design excellence by British architects is more than three men thick, to paraphrase W.R. Lethaby.

It is perhaps less well known that it is the work of younger generations of architects and designers that has significantly contributed to the strength of the British architectural reputation both at home and abroad; Alsop and Störmer, Jan Kaplicky, Rick Mather, Eva Jiricna, David Chipperfield, Jestico and Whiles are some of the practices to be reckoned with, as this survey shows.

In this book Noel Moffett has attempted a survey of what he considers to be 'the best' of British architecture over the past decade or so. He also seeks to extend the conceptual and philosophical framework of this work in a predictive fashion into the 21st century.

Noel Moffett is no martyr to Modernism. He does, however, retain his original intellectual commitment to the Modern Movement's main tenets; after all he was for a time an assistant to Serge Chermayeff among others. In this book he often recalls with relish his original commitment – when he was a young man – to the fundamental ideologies of Modernism in Britain. However, as with much of his own work his selective view of others' efforts is tempered with both courtesy and good taste. He shows a sense of fairness and seeks out talent, as he has exhibited elsewhere throughout his working life, both as a practitioner and an architectural teacher and lecturer. He has promoted the best of British architecture in many parts of the world.

It is therefore not surprising to see that in the compilation of this original book Noel Moffett – like his Modern Movement progenitors – delights in categorization and what they might have loosely referred to as 'zoning'. Thus, he adopts a rather Modernist approach in delineating the various pluralities he sees at work in contemporary architectural developments. In the book he provides ten categories or 'directions', some of which overlap, others of which are so controversial as to open up a whole area of discussion and debate and even, as in my own case, possible disagreements! Be that as it may, the structure provided prevents the more conventional and somewhat tedious, stylistic references and provides 'functional' areas into which the author's own comments can be lodged. It results of course in a thoroughly subjective interpretation but one which draws on lively concepts and interpretations, particularly framed within the categorical modes adopted.

The book itself is fashioned on an earlier publication that Noel Moffett and his wife, the architect Alina Moffett, prepared for SARP, the Association of Polish Architects, for a special issue of their magazine *Architektura* (No. 6, 1988) subtitled *Architektura Brytyjska lat osiemdziesiatych* (loosely translated as 'British Architecture of the Eighties'). It provided an extensive survey of British architectural achievements at the time of its compilation, 1986–87. Although poorly printed, much delayed in its publication and even rather badly edited, the magazine issue provided some unique insights into British architectural trends.

Since its publication, however, a number of further books have now appeared on British architecture of the 1980s but few share the wide spectrum displayed in Noel Moffett's work. Although the original publication in Polish had a somewhat restricted circulation and its publication hardly compensated for the immense effort of work that the author put into it, like Topsy it continued to grow. So did the sheer volume of 'good' buildings by British architects, both nationally and abroad. This book therefore should be welcomed because it offers a comprehensive view of British architecture, yet one viewed through experienced eyes and tempered by an intimate knowledge of many of the structures mentioned.

Dennis Sharp, 1991

The Crystal Palace under construction

Colin Stansfield Smith's Farnborough College of Technology

Gordon Wilson's Princess of Wales conservatory at Kew Gardens

# INTRODUCTION

Sir Joseph Paxton designed that extraordinary building the Crystal Palace 140 years ago — and architecture's Modern Movement was born. I often wonder, were he alive today, what he would say about the state of British architecture at the end of the 20th century.

## 1980 TO 1990

A quick look at the 1980s shows Modernism struggling on and adapting to a changing society, Post-modernism slowly disappearing, hi-tech thriving, Classical Revivalism spreading, Historicism gaining strength, Façadism pushing up above ground, Eclecticism ubiquitous, the birth of Deconstruction, the puberty of Community Architecture; it also shows architects moving in many directions (this book suggests ten), too much commercialism and — in the most unlikely places — four (or perhaps five) examples of hi-tech brilliance.

I can't imagine Paxton being very kind to our Classical Revivalists or to our Façadists, or showing much sympathy with the Prince of Wales' 'Vision of Britain'; but a few of our High-Tech buildings would surely delight him.

Jonathan Glancey's book *New British Architecture* (published in 1989) is an interesting comment on what some of our more adventurous architects built during the 1980s. In it he reminds us that:

'the main change during the 1980s has been a political one. The shift in patronage from the public to the private sector, and the increasing emphasis placed on industrial achievement and private wealth has inevitably changed the face of British architecture.'

Happily, however, a few public sector architects have fought valiantly against this trend and, noticeably, Colin Stansfield Smith (Hampshire County Architect) and Gordon Wilson (Property Services Agency) have designed buildings of the very highest standard.

The other main change during the 1980s has been a three-pronged technological one: 'fast-track', CAD and fax. Some of our big developers commissioned American architects who had already learned, with the aid of computers, not only to design with great speed but also to turn out drawings at great speed and to organize building contracts with efficiency and understanding of business methods. These skills, combined with modern methods of communication (especially fax), helped to solve the complex many-faceted problems involved in the design of many modern buildings.

Unfortunately fast-track does not encourage — on the part of the architect — the development of contextual

Office blocks at Canary Wharf, London Docklands

Housing at Shadwell Basin, London Docklands

Sir Norman Foster's Hong Kong bank

sensitivity or intuitive artistic expression or even creative draughtsmanship. It is a sad comment on the society of the 1980s that many architects could not find the time to design in the way they wished. Cesar Pelli's huge office block at Canary Wharf in London's docklands was designed and built in a shorter time than many better buildings one-tenth of its size. It is revealing, however, to compare its design with that of a housing scheme by MacCormac Jamieson Prichard just a few docks away from it: the first of them, which would fit snugly into a Manhattan context, is contextually incongruous on the Isle of Dogs and totally out of scale with London town; the other not only satisfies the housing needs and expectations of the local people but is also sensitively and skilfully related to its dock site: an architecture specifically designed for a site with very particular characteristics, echoing the scale and quality of the original warehouse buildings – convincing dockland architecture, in fact. The historian Nikolaus Pevsner who wrote eloquently about 'the Englishness of English architecture' would have strongly condemned the Canary Wharf development.

The Canary Wharf buildings and others in docklands are situated in an 'enterprise zone' created by the Government to encourage developers to develop there – where planning permission is not required. As I watch the Canary Wharf buildings in particular lift their unwelcome bulk above the London skyline I am reminded of one of the Athens Charter's precepts: 'Architecture detached from the serious problems of its time is not good architecture.'

Actually a few British architects solved these problems well. We cannot but admire, for example, Sir Norman Foster's achievement in honouring the undertaking he gave his client to design and build the huge Hong Kong bank – at the other side of the world – in an incredibly short time (six years). The problems of context and scale – as this book demonstrates – have also been solved, sometimes with both sensitivity and wit, by Sir Norman Foster, Nicholas Grimshaw, Ralph Erskine and Michael Hopkins (outstandingly in his Mound stand at Lord's cricket ground). But some architects have been over-concerned with elevational elaboration and this has led to 1980s architecture's being labelled 'a battle of the styles', with buildings placed in one category or another based on style.

Mound stand at Lord's cricket ground

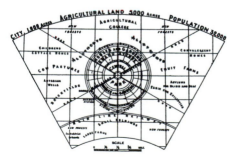
Ebenezer Howard's ideal town diagram

## 1990 TO 2000

And what of the 1990s? To get a glimpse of the best of our 1990s architecture I think we must look back to the 19th century and the work of Joseph Paxton and the great railway engineers Brunel and Telford, and also to the 1930s – particularly to CIAM and the Athens charter.

CIAM was a series of international conferences where architects discussed at length the problems of the day – sociological, philosophical and technical. The Athens Charter was a manifesto which set down, with great conviction, the aims and ambitions of the Modern Movement in architecture; it became the bible of the early modernists.

The novels of Dickens and the drawings of Hogarth had awakened the social conscience of the Victorians to the appalling conditions under which most people lived and worked; Paxton had shown – way back in the 1850s – how mass-production and prefabrication could be harnessed to create buildings of convenience and beauty; at the turn of the century Ebenezer Howard's book *Tomorrow* was the blueprint for 26 British new towns which gave people a better living and working environment; and in 1933 the Athens Charter stated categorically that it was the duty of every architect

'to clear the slums, to let the sun into every room in the house and the workshop, to put a green belt round every city and introduce a new era of air and light and green space.'

But World War II came, with its ruthless bombing of cities and wholesale destruction of homes and workplaces. After the war, in the name of 'comprehensive redevelopment', we bulldozed the centres of our cities – destroying many old well-loved buildings in the process – and left them empty and derelict. The people whose homes were destroyed considered this too high a price to pay for the new image of architecture and the city and turned against the architects and the planners. Who can blame them?

But we didn't listen to their criticism and complaints. In the interests of providing as many homes as quickly as possible we built huge inhuman housing estates which people hated, and tall blocks of flats which most people could not accept – especially families with young children. To satisfy our developer clients' demands for more and more office space we built gaunt rectangular steel-and-glass office blocks – pushing up against the skyline like very sore thumbs.

And so we became unpopular with the public. And we still are. Hence Façadism and Classical Revival and the Prince of Wales.

In the early years of the 1990s the great debate intensified: Modern versus Classical. Thanks to the powerful influence of the Prince, architecture had become a popular subject for discussion –

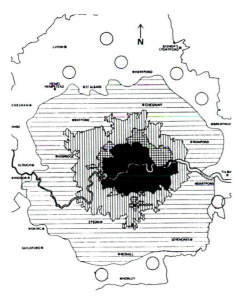

Shopping centre at Milton Keynes, the last of the new towns

Greater London, with its green belt and the new towns surrounding it

Post-war office blocks in London

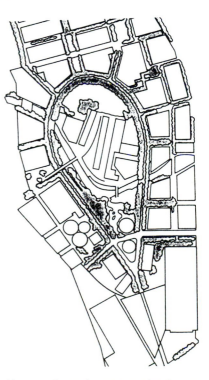

Sir Norman Foster's master plan for an urban park at King's Cross, London

Zaha Hadid's office building in Berlin (designed but not built)

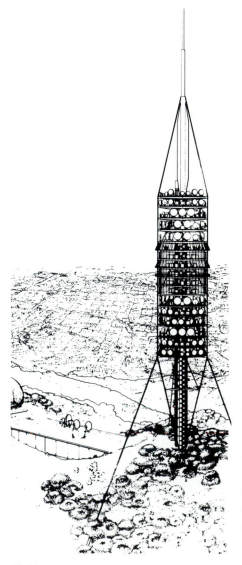

Sir Norman Foster's telecommunications tower in Barcelona

at all levels – and some developers had realized the advantages of commissioning designs from architects whose work was acceptable to the Prince.

The controversy over the way in which three major London sites should be developed has raged for several years and, as I write, it seems almost certain that Paternoster Square (north of St Paul's cathedral) and Spitalfields (East London's former market area) will be redeveloped in a neo-Classical manner. The third site at King's Cross – largely because of Sir Norman Foster's design skills and persuasive talents – will see a fine example of modern urban design and landscaping, if it is built in accordance with his master plan; it will give this part of central London a badly needed urban park, major office, housing and shopping accommodation and will include the Channel Tunnel rail terminal.

When Pevsner wrote about the Englishness of English architecture he described London like this:

'The essential qualities . . . are closeness, variety and intricacy, and the ever-recurring contrasts of tall and low, of large and small, of wide and narrow, of straight and crooked, the closes and retreats and odd leafy corners. All this a modern plan can keep – not preserve, but recreate, and combine with the amenities of the 20th century.'

All through the 1980s and well into the 1990s the battle of the styles continued here in Britain and many architects have been over-concerned with pleasing the public; but none the less the era has seen some fine new works of architecture capable of taking their place among this country's finest achievements. There is no doubt in my mind that the best British buildings in this hectic eclectic age are those that use today's evolving technology to solve today's problems and satisfy today's needs, and those that conform to Pevsner's specification while at the same time looking back to our history and learning from it – but not copying it. The precepts of the Athens Charter make as much sense in our fast-moving rapidly changing society as they did in the 1930s, but they have been modified and adapted convincingly and sometimes brilliantly by our best architects.

As the 21st century approaches, British architecture is in a chaotic, rather interesting state: some of our architects are looking back, with the Prince, and hoping that ancient Greece and Rome will help them to solve our contemporary problems and thereby make them more popular with the public; some of them are learning from Las Vegas and are decorating their sheds; some of them (perhaps the best) are using today's technology to create new exciting forms and structures; and some of our younger architects – unappreciated as yet in Britain – are designing stimulating innovative buildings overseas, especially in Germany and Japan. It is particularly interesting, I think, that British architects (young and old) are designing significant airport buildings around the world – in London, Nice and Hong Kong.

# 1
# MODIFIED MODERN

The Athens Charterists enunciated a series of design principles which guided the development of the Modern Movement in the 1930s and has in fact continued to do so ever since. For most architects anxious to create a better world and a better environment in which people could live and work it made a lot of sense: to clear the slums, let the sun into every room in the house, put a green belt round every city (to prevent indiscriminate suburban expansion) and introduce a new era of light and air and green spaces. Unfortunately much of what was built – especially tall point blocks of flats and office blocks clad with glass curtain walling – was very unpopular with the public.

Today life is more complex and much of the environment more urban and more dense than it was when the Athens Charterists wrote their manifesto. Many architects – perhaps the majority of them – have therefore modified these principles to suit the changed and changing situation and to counteract the severe criticism by the public of the design of many modern buildings.

And so the design of many of our new buildings today is richer, more flexible and more acceptable to the people who use them than it used to be. The Modern Movement has been brought up to date and been given a more human face.

Living room in a West London flat

# BETHNAL GREEN HEALTH CENTRE • LONDON

## AVANTI ARCHITECTS

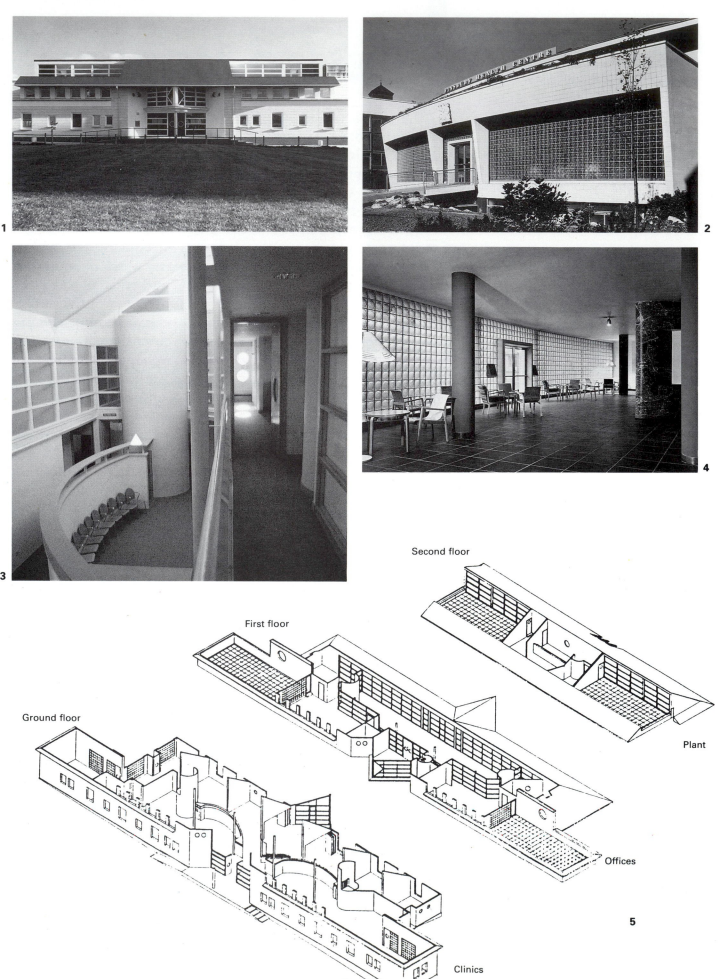

1

2

3

4

Second floor

First floor

Ground floor

Plant

Offices

Clinics

5

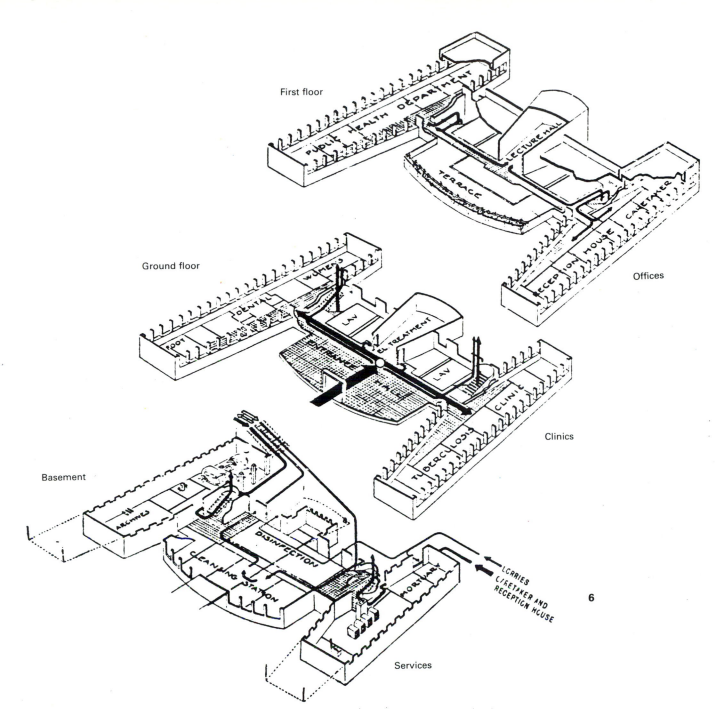

First floor

Ground floor

Basement

Offices

Clinics

Services

6

1 Entrance elevation of the Bethnal Green Health Centre
2 Entrance elevation of the Finsbury Health Centre
3 Entrance hall: Bethnal Green
4 Entrance hall: Finsbury
5 Floor plans: Bethnal Green
6 Floor plans: Finsbury

When the *Architectural Review* published (in June 1988) details of the design of this building they had this to say:

**'Bethnal Green Health Centre is in one of the poorest parts of London. Its clients are of many different backgrounds, languages and cultures. The architects (Avanti) were faced with the task of creating a public building which had to make its presence felt, and yet which could be reassuring to people in distress. John Allan, the chief designer, is a devotee of Lubetkin's work. He writes perceptively of his hero's Finsbury Health Centre, one of the canonical buildings of British Modernism which exploited the new-found powers of construction to fulfil a clear social programme. Bethnal Green is a conscious successor to Finsbury.'**

It is interesting and rewarding, I think, to compare the design of the two buildings, separated in time by 50 years: the same attitude to design, the same planning articulation, the same welcoming entrance hall.

The new health centre was completed in late 1988.

# EASTLEIGH HOSTEL FOR THE PHYSICALLY HANDICAPPED •
## HAMPSHIRE

COLIN STANSFIELD SMITH (Hampshire County Architect)

A 24-place hostel with six sheltered housing units. It is a rehabilitation centre, with a central kitchen and laundry, shopping and hairdressing facilities, a bar, a lounge and a large communal meeting room. Linked banked accommodation is located on either side of a brick-paved street. Load-bearing brick walls support a light steel roof structure.

Built in 1985.

**1** Plan
**2** Interior street

# FLEMING FULTON SCHOOL • MALONE ROAD • BELFAST
## KENNEDY, FITZGERALD & ASSOCIATES

1

This comprehensive school for the disabled is typical of the excellent social service being given to the people of Northern Ireland. Much of the accommodation is used by the local community outside school hours. It has teaching and multi-purpose areas, a swimming pool, gymnasium and workshop. The multi-purpose hall and youth club form the 'social centre' to the complex and are surrounded by remedial and special subject-teaching areas grouped around landscaped courtyards and terraces.
  Built in 1983.

1 General view
2 Playground
3 Floor plans
4 Sections

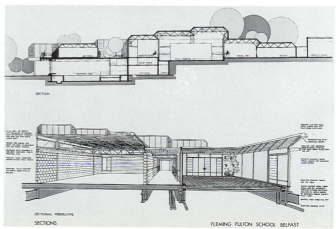

2

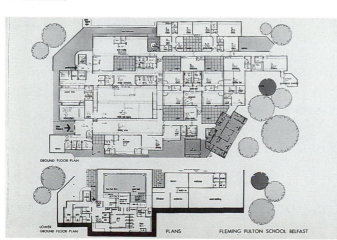

3

4

5

# MAIDSTONE HOSPITAL • KENT

## POWELL MOYA & PARTNERS

Built in 1983, here is a classic example of how the monumental scale of a very large hospital can be reduced by skilful planning. The architects have created a series of 'nuclear' two-storey ward units, each of them overlooking a landscaped court – all linked together by wide glazed corridors.

The hospital can be extended in three directions merely by adding more planning modules.

1 General view
2 Site layout
3 Hospital entrance
4 Typical interior

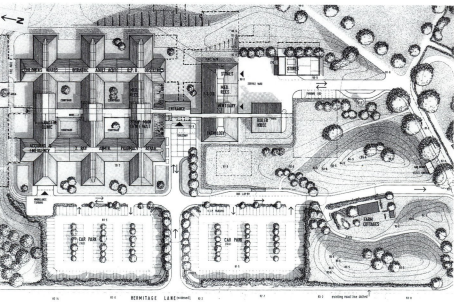

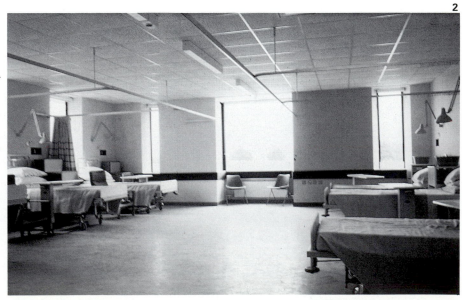

# STERLING HOTEL • HEATHROW AIRPORT • WEST LONDON
## MANSER ASSOCIATES

1

2

Michael Manser has designed a most dramatic and unusual parallelogram-shaped 400-bed hotel situated close to Heathrow Airport's Terminal 4. The strong shape of the building was suggested partly by the maze of airport access roads, partly by the need to provide a clear visible presence to traffic on the A30 (the main road from London) and partly to enable both early morning sun to reach into the atrium between the parallel bedroom blocks and the late evening sun into the area occupied by restaurants and bars.

The design concept is essentially inward-looking, but perhaps the most interesting feature of the design is the way in which the central area opens out on two sides, allowing soft landscape to enter into the heart of the building.

The hotel was opened in 1990.

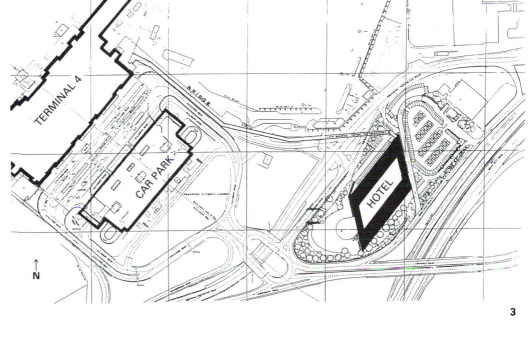

3

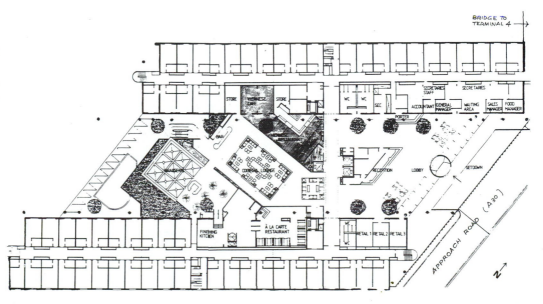

4

**1** General view
**2** Atrium
**3** Site plan
**4** Ground-floor plan

# EPSOM RACECOURSE, THE QUEEN'S STAND • SURREY
## RICHARD HORDEN ASSOCIATES

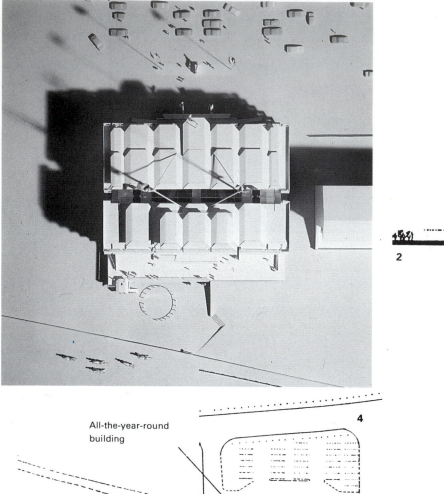

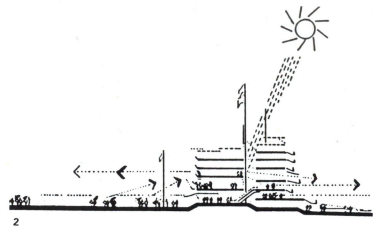

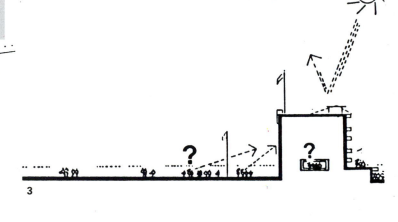

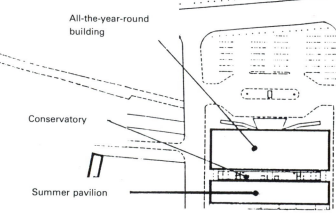

All-the-year-round building

Conservatory

Summer pavilion

The Epsom stand, built in 1992, has three distinct elements: the 'all-the-year-round building', with reception, exhibition space, restaurants and administrative offices; the 'summer pavilion' designed for race viewing, with stewards' and jockeys' facilities, Royal suite, private boxes and balconies; and, between the two pavilions, the 'conservatory' – a spacious, glass-walled area, with lifts and staircases, escalators and balconies, and with fine views of the Downs from within the heart of the building.

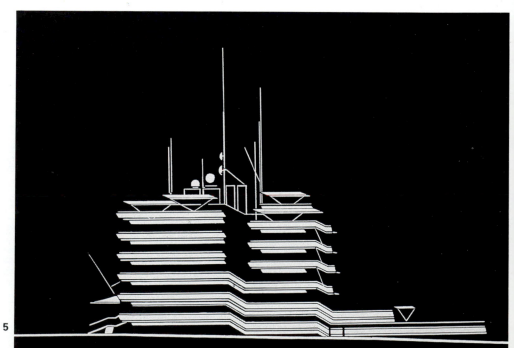

**1** Aerial view of model
**2/3** Architect's design sketches
**4** Site plan
**5** General view

# THE ISMAILI CENTRE • SOUTH KENSINGTON • LONDON

## CASSON CONDER PARTNERSHIP

Designed in 1983 for London's Ismaili Muslim community, this building provides its religious, cultural and social needs. On an island site opposite the imposing Victoria and Albert Museum it has a strong sculptural form with an attractive garden on the roof.

1 Site plan
2 General view
3 First-floor plan
4 Section

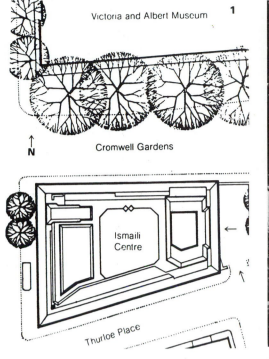

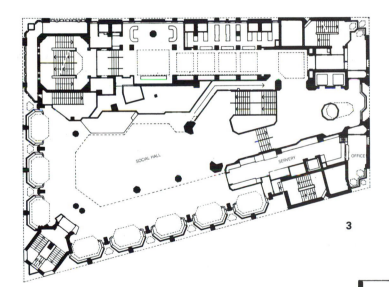

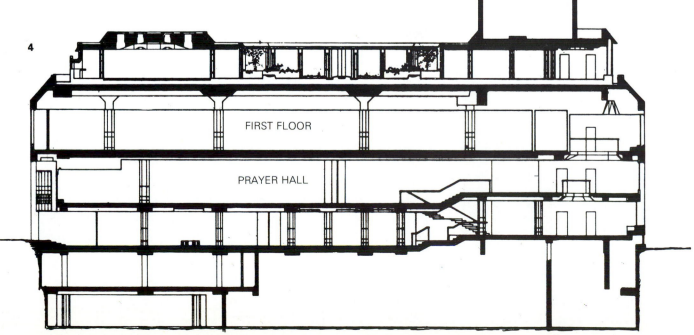

# ROYAL CONCERT HALL · NOTTINGHAM
## RENTON HOWARD WOOD LEVIN

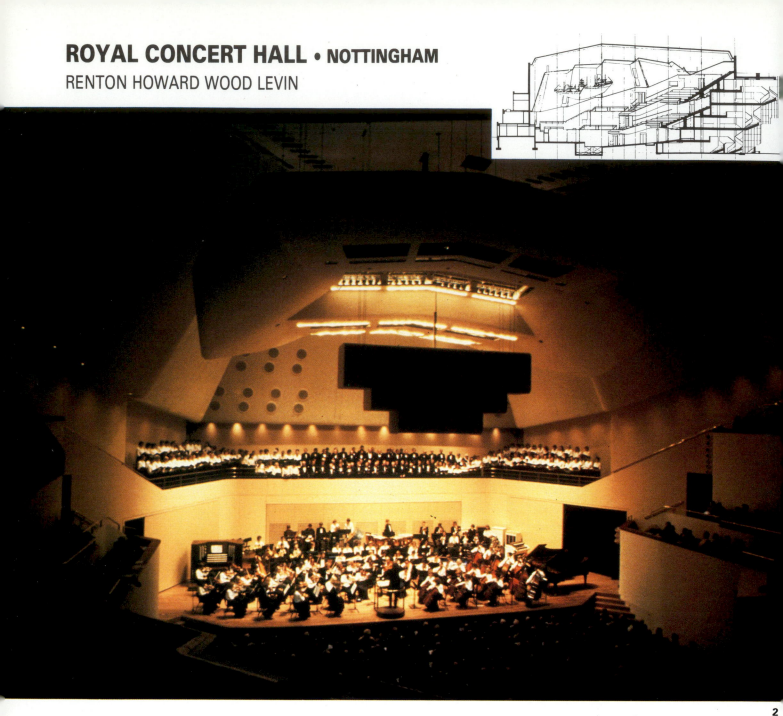

Nottingham's concert hall is a multi-purpose building designed (in 1982) for symphony concerts, conferences, cinema, trade shows and wrestling. Flexible staging, retractable seating tiers and a large orchestra pit combine with acoustic adjustability to provide suitable settings for the full musical and dance spectrum, through to hard rock.

**1** Section **2** Auditorium **3** Entrance elevation **4** Ground-floor

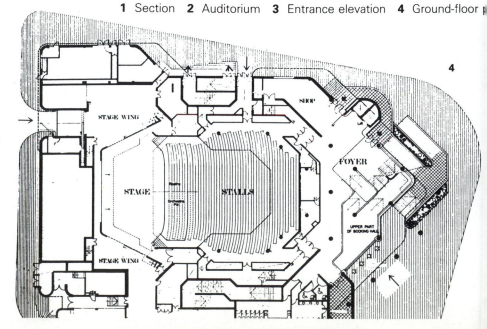

# GROUP PRACTICE SURGERY • HIGHGATE • NORTH LONDON
## STEPHEN GAGE OF DOUGLAS STEPHEN & PARTNERS

**1**

This surgery was designed (in 1988) for a group practice working in close association with a new community care building nearby. The site is very narrow and deep and this has prompted the creation of a pleasant glazed courtyard which is in fact the patients' waiting area. This is the major feature of the design.

The architecture is intentionally simple, calm and relaxed, and fittings and finishes have been carefully chosen to be non-institutional.

**1** Entrance elevation
**2** Cross-section
**3** Internal courtyard
**4** Ground-floor plan

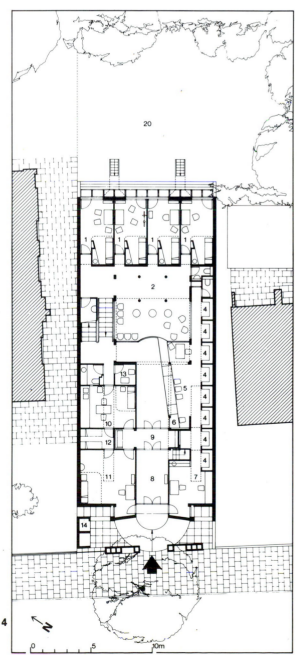

# CLIMATIC RESEARCH BUILDING · UNIVERSITY OF EAST ANGLIA · NORWICH

## RICK MATHER

1

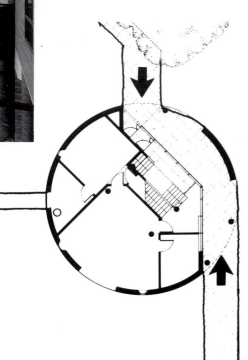

2

Rick Mather's research building at the University of East Anglia's School of Education acts as a 'gateway' defining the route from the campus entrance to Sir Norman Foster's Sainsbury Arts Centre. The building has a fine lofty entrance hall, major public areas and a courtyard garden for outdoor teaching.

Phase one (illustrated here) was completed in 1985.

3

1 Interior
2 Ground-floor plan
3 General view
4 Axonometric
5 Plan and perspective sketch of entrance hall

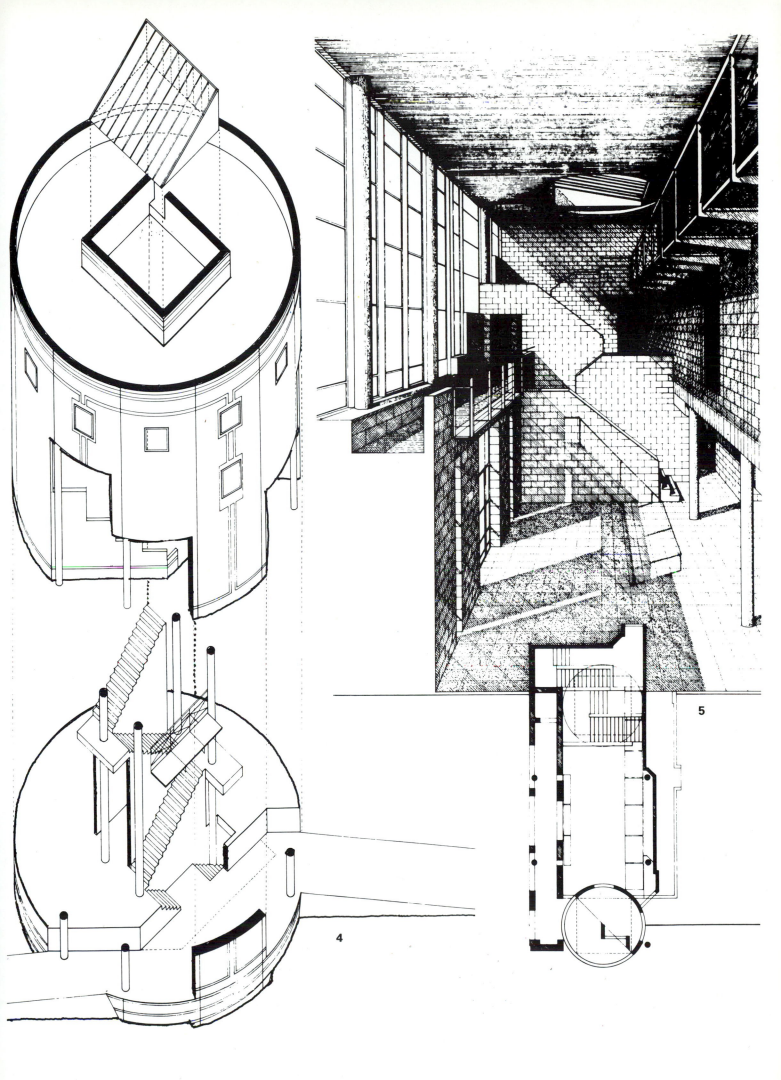

4

5

# TRINIDAD AND TOBAGO HALL OF JUSTICE • WEST INDIES

## HOWELL KILLICK PARTRIDGE & AMIS

This building which now dominates the main square of Port of Spain has 28 courtrooms, two large libraries and a convocation hall seating 500. The architectural concept is generated from a symmetrical first-floor plan where 16 courts are disposed round the perimeter, with public circulation in a central hall.

The reinforced concrete structure is designed to high seismic standards. The two main steel staircases are hung from the concrete roof structure.

The Hall of Justice was built in 1985.

**1** General view from the Square
**2** Location plan and two sections
**3** First-floor plan

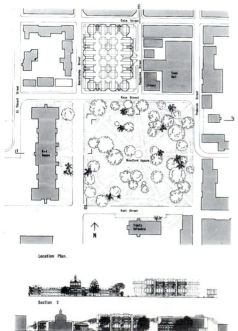

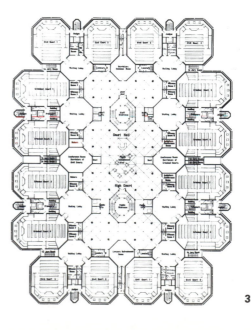

14

# EUROPEAN INVESTMENT BANK · LUXEMBOURG

## DENYS LASDUN & PARTNERS

Sir Denys Lasdun in 1981, designed this headquarters building in Luxembourg for the European Investment Bank. The extended arms of its low-lying cruciform shape define four distinct spaces: conference facilities, sports facilities, staff restaurant and main entrance. The conference facilities are given pride of place, with panoramic views over woods, valleys and distant city.

**1** Conference foyer
**2** Site layout
  A Forecourt
  B Restaurant quadrant
  C Conference quadrant
  D Sports quadrant
**3** View from the south-east

# WHITEFRIARS OFFICE BUILDING · FLEET STREET · LONDON

## YRM PARTNERSHIP

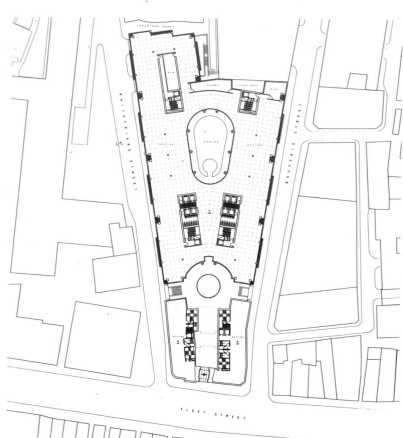

1 **Typical elevation**
2 **First-floor plan**
3 **Atrium**
4 **Aerial view of model (from Fleet Street)**

YRM's office building symbolizes the recent change of use of buildings in London's Fleet Street from newspaper offices and printing works to financial services offices. It respects the historic character of the area, retains the Fleet Street façades, the listed Tipperary pub and the mediaeval Ashentree court, and creates a pedestrian street linking these old buildings and Fleet Street to the new offices. A large eight-storey atrium acts as a visual climax to the approach from Fleet Street and gives good daylight both to the upper office floors and to the extra-high trading floors below.

Built 1988–89.

# CIVIC CENTRE AT CHESTER-LE-STREET • DURHAM
## FAULKNER BROWNS ARCHITECTS

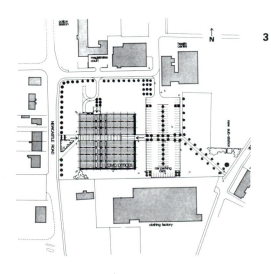

A continuous dialogue between public and local authority is encouraged by the creation of a glazed spine walkway through the new building which contains all the local authority offices and continues outside the building linking it to existing civic buildings. An elegant sophisticated design, with steel used imaginatively — both as structure and in the detail design of fittings and furniture.

Built in 1982.

ground floor plan

car park

A  Treasurer
B  Technical
C  Restaurant
D  Kitchen
E  Carpark

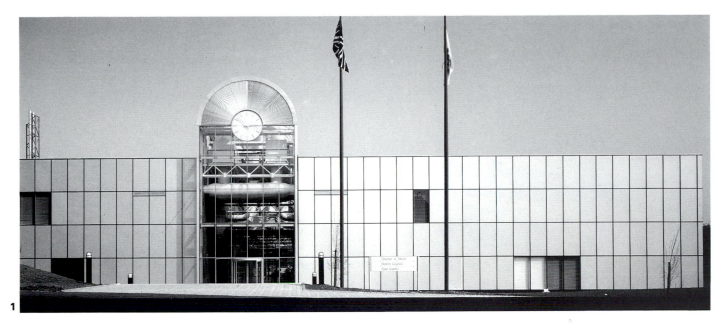

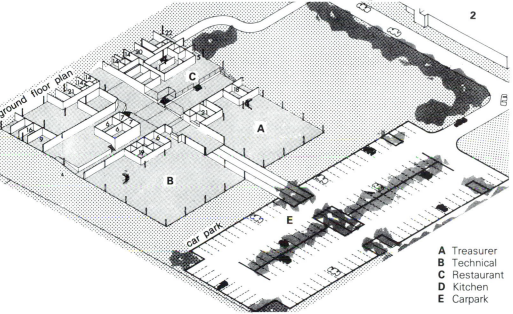

1  Entrance elevation
2  Ground-floor isometric
3  Site plan
4  A typical interior

# MÜNSTER LIBRARY • GERMANY

## ARCHITEKTURBÜRO BOLLES-WILSON

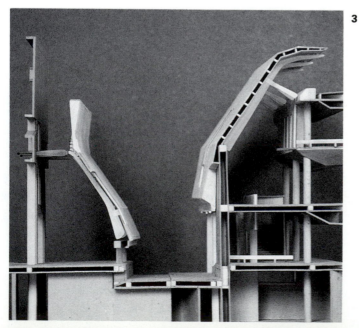

1

2

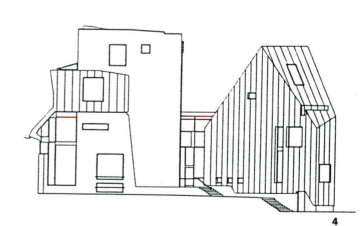

3

4

This interesting, rather complex design for Münster's library won a major competition in the late 1980s and now, in the early 1990s, is under construction.

It is a clever solution to a difficult problem on an awkward site bisected by a public pedestrian walkway. The architects have solved the problem quite ingeniously by placing the main reading rooms and book stacks in a wedge-shaped building (half-a-boat in fact, reminiscent of Peter Wilson's love of boats), and the reception and ancillary accommodation in a separate building on the other side of the walkway. The two buildings are connected by an upper-level bridge and also at basement level.

Built 1991–94.

1 General view
2 Cross-section
3 Structure model
4 Elevation
5 Lower-floor plan
6 Longitudinal section

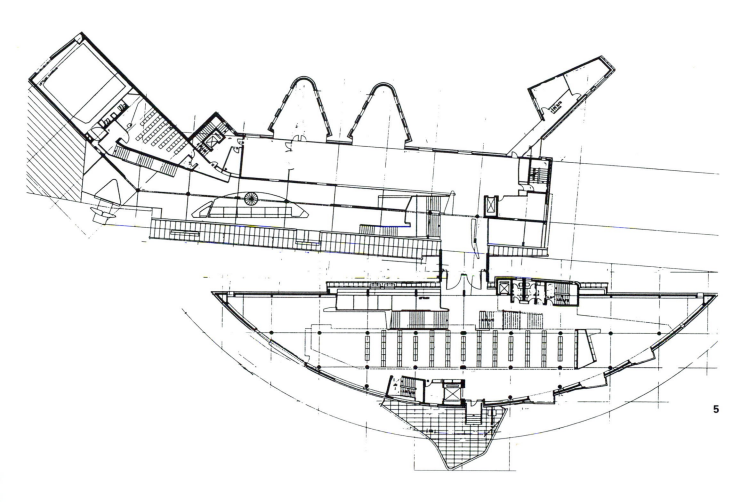

5

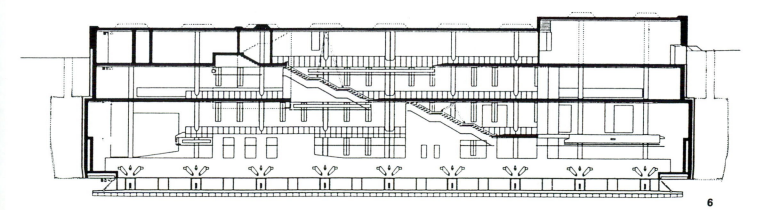

6

19

# HOUSING AT BERGAMO · NORTH ITALY

## NEAVE BROWN & DAVID PORTER

1

2

Three apartment blocks on three adjoining sites form an incomplete square. The blocks are arranged about a central garden in a compositional play of symmetries and asymmetries. The 'outside' outside presents a wall to the street. The 'inside' outside opens tiers of terraces towards the garden. Entries and stairs reach from the garden to the core of the blocks where a circular stair joins all floors to the garages below. The garage is a grotto, sheltered but partly open to the sky, light and shade: not a cellar. From the ascending terraces the garden appears complete, poaching space, trees and shade from the neighbour.

The apartment blocks were built in 1989.

**1** General view
**2** Ground-floor plan
**3** Axonometric

3

# URBAN REDEVELOPMENT • BROADGATE • LONDON
## ARUP ASSOCIATES

In the best tradition of modern urban planning, Arups have created – next door to Liverpool Street Station – two fine new public pedestrian spaces, with high-rise high-density office buildings overlooking them. Both are already popular with the public; one (circular) is an ice-skating rink in winter and an urban park arena in summer; together they form a sophisticated pedestrian link between two busy traffic streets.

This is phases 1 to 4 of a 14-phase project. It is to be hoped that future phases – designed by other architects – will maintain Arup's high standard.

Built 1985–88.

**1** Aerial view
**2** Circular arena

# APPLE COMPUTER BUILDING • STOCKLEY PARK • WEST LONDON

TROUGHTON McASLAN

This is the first phase of Apple Computers' British headquarters located in the expanding Stockley Park business park 15 miles west of central London. Built in 1989, the building is organized on two floors along the length of a central double-height circulating gallery formed by a light well at first-floor level and creating an internal street at ground floor. The upper floor provides offices and open-plan workstations. The entrance to the building is from a fully glazed tower leading directly into the landscaped atrium, with meeting rooms and training facilities and with coffee spaces and restaurant off it.

Externally the envelope consists of semi-translucent insulating panels and clear glass shaded to the south by tensioned sunscreens at first-floor level. The roof profile consists of two shallow barrel-vaulted wings, with the rooflight and mechanical plant located in the central section of the roof and organized along the building's length. The external sunblinds help to soften a rather austere but elegant shed.

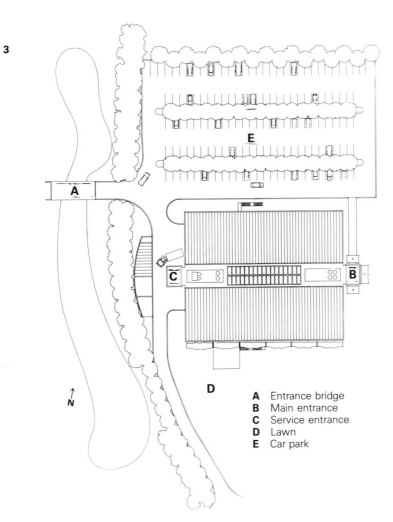

3

↑
N

A  Entrance bridge
B  Main entrance
C  Service entrance
D  Lawn
E  Car park

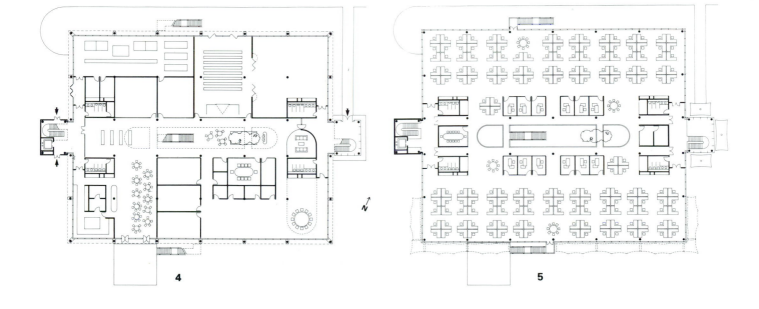

4

5

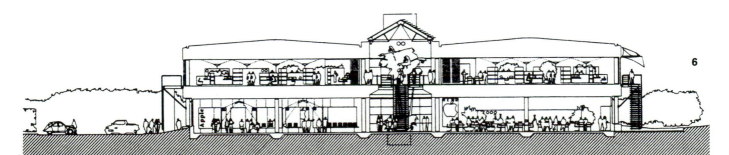

6

23

# 'TOKYO FORUM' COMPETITION ENTRY • 1985

## SIR JAMES STIRLING, MICHAEL WILFORD & ASSOCIATES

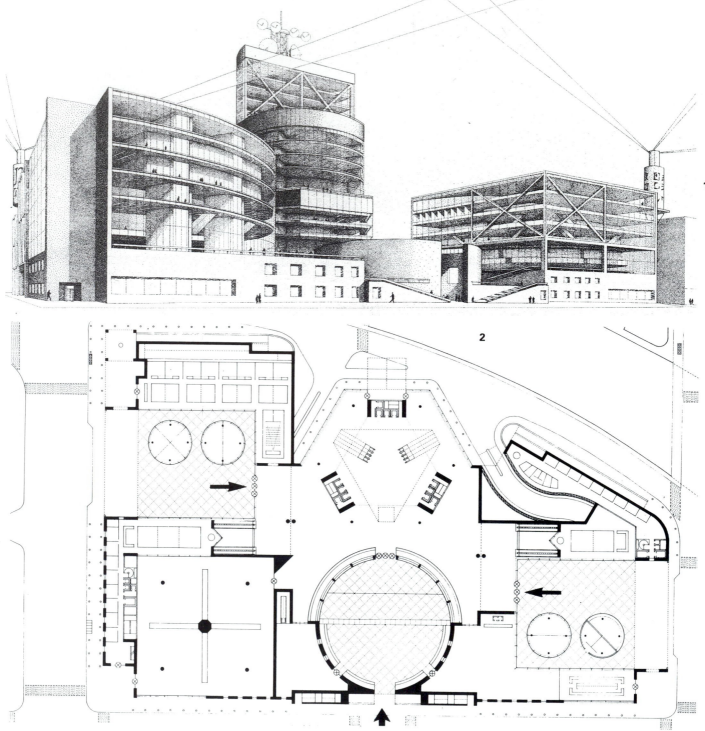

The architects' proposal for this cultural centre emphasizes the symbolic importance of the complex by placing a tall building in the centre, related to an outdoor public courtyard enclosed by a stone wall — reminiscent of the very popular courtyard at Stuttgart's Staatsgalerie. Lower but equally monumental buildings are placed at each side. The transparency of the buildings is both a sophisticated interpretation of *glasarchitektur* and an expression of the new building and servicing technologies. Searchlights, lasers and 'fantastic' components contribute to this association. The major volumes are designed as separate forms connected by the dominant base of the buildings which contains the information exchanges, gallery and central common lobby.

Here is 'modern architecture' at its best — modified to embrace richness and three-dimensional excitement; here is the marriage of sculpture and architecture.

# KOBE INSTITUTE • JAPAN
## TROUGHTON McASLAN (Architects), OVE ARUP PARTNERSHIP (Engineers)

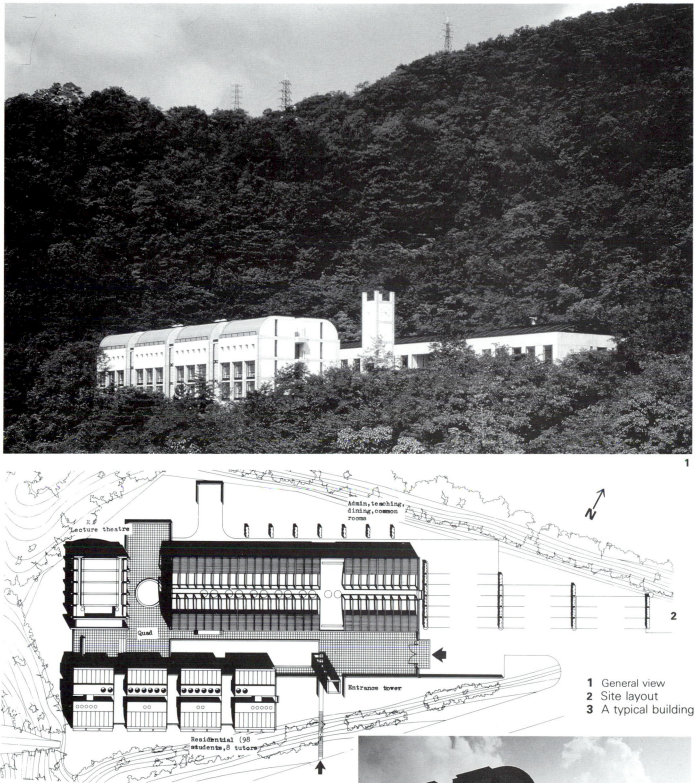

1

Admin, teaching, dining, common rooms

Lecture theatre

Quad

Entrance tower

Residential (98 students, 8 tutors

N

2

1 General view
2 Site layout
3 A typical building

The Kobe Institute was founded by St Catherine's College, Oxford, to further relations between Europe and Japan. It offers a one-year course in arts and science to graduates of Japanese universities, with lectures in English by tutors from St Catherine's. Teaching and residential accommodation is provided in a series of buildings grouped — in the traditional Oxford manner — around a quad, in this case rather long and narrow. The architects were commissioned in July 1990, construction began in December 1990 and the Institute was completed, on schedule, in August 1991 — an astonishing achievement.

3

# 2
# VERNACULAR MODERN

'Why do you want to photograph that monstrosity?' said a passer-by when he saw me photographing a small office block in Windsor which we had designed. Because it was very close to Windsor Castle – a great gaunt building – we had given our building a rugged appearance by exposing the concrete frame (with an exposed aggregate finish) and using second-hand bricks, with raked-out joints, for wall construction.

Our critic didn't like our building because it looked unfamiliar: it had a flat roof, when he would have preferred a pitched one covered with slates or tiles; he thought that concrete surfaces should be covered, not exposed. Familiarity seems to be most people's criterion for good architecture. They will accept high technology in steel or concrete for airports or ferry terminals because there is no strong tradition for the design of these buildings. But the designers of houses, churches and small office blocks next door to castles must pay attention to the British vernacular, which is brickwork, pitched roofs with slates or tiles, and timber windows.

Actually the Robert Matthew Johnson Marshall Partnership showed how to do it some years ago at Hillingdon when they designed new civic offices for the Borough and gave them everything the traditionalists could wish for; and Broadway Malyan did it interestingly at Bexleyheath in Kent in 1989 in the same way.

The best modern vernacular work is being designed today outside the London area, often by city architects and their staffs. It is quite a joy to walk through a new housing scheme in York, Norwich or Milton Keynes and admire the skill with which the architects have solved the problem – and to notice the obvious contentment of the families recently come to live in these houses.

The Shambles, York

# CLOVELLY VISITORS' CENTRE • DEVON

## VAN HEYNINGEN AND HAWARD

The architects have here been strongly influenced by the character and tradition of the architecture of Clovelly, an old fishing village on the north Devon coast, with its very steep and narrow streets and its simple direct use of local building materials. In their visitors' centre, located a little distance from the village, they have used the same materials for walls and roof but have added more sophisticated ones – steel and PVC. The long horizontal line of the roof emphasizes the role played by the building as a gateway to the village, and its success as a contemporary building is assured by the importance given to the long access ramp and the magnificent views of the sea-coast from the restaurant.
Built in 1988.

**1** General view
**2** Sketch of coast and village
**3** Section
**4** Plan
**5** Restaurant interior (opposite)

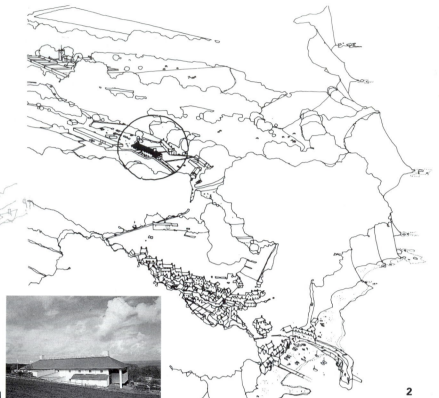

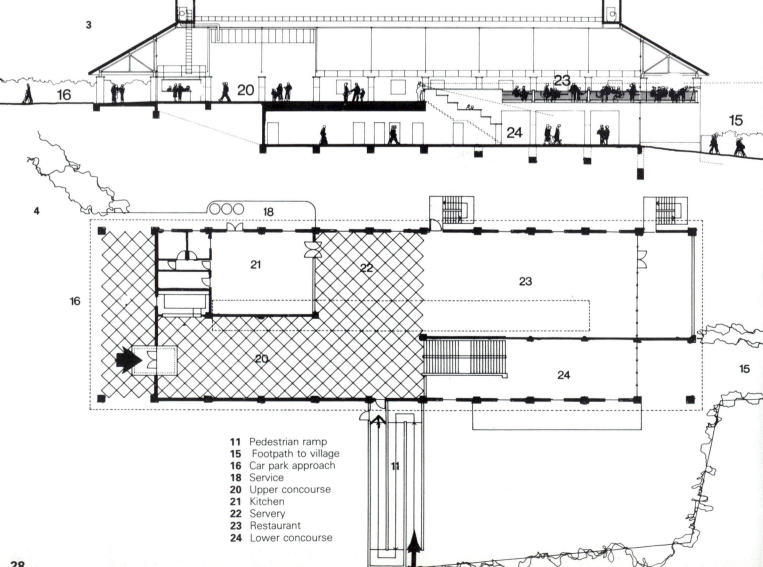

**11** Pedestrian ramp
**15** Footpath to village
**16** Car park approach
**18** Service
**20** Upper concourse
**21** Kitchen
**22** Servery
**23** Restaurant
**24** Lower concourse

# WATERSPORTS CENTRE • LONDON DOCKLANDS
## KIT ALLSOPP ARCHITECTS

Kit Allsopp's well-planned building is dominated by a
huge roof which actually extends well beyond the
perimeter of the building to give outdoor covered space
for boats and boatmen alike. The roof, with its overtones
of shed, temple and Tyrolean hotel, is a most successful
visual stop to a long stretch of docklands water.
 Built in 1989.

1 General view
2 First-floor plan
3 Ground-floor plan
4 East elevation, with original docklands crane

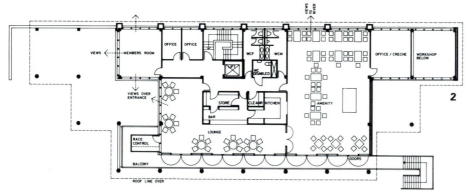

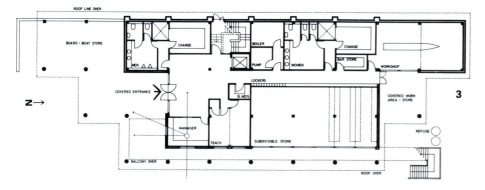

# COTTAGE NEAR LLANDEILO • DYFED • SOUTH WALES

## ALINA AND NOEL MOFFETT

The client for this small country house in south Wales was a model-maker who asked the architects 'to reinterpret the traditional Welsh way of using local materials'. The house was designed (in 1985) to take advantage of magnificent distant views of the Brecon Beacons mountains. A glazed studio links it to an existing barn converted to workshop and garage use. A sloping stone chimney stack contains an outside fire-place (opening on to the terrace) and visually separates the living and sleeping areas of the house.

**1** General view from the south-east
**2** Longitudinal section
**3** Aerial view of the model
**4** Plan

1

2

3

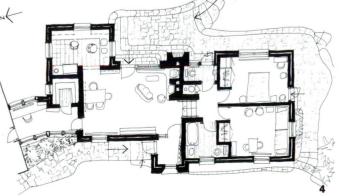

4

# PENPLAS HOUSING • SWANSEA • SOUTH WALES
## PCKO ARCHITECTS

1

This housing scheme for Swansea was the winner in a major design competition in 1989. The architects have based their design on a typical traditional village scene in south Wales. It has four elements: a street of varying widths, a village square, a cluster of a few houses, and a formal group of houses set back from the street.

**1** A typical group of houses
**2** Site layout
**3** Typical floor plans

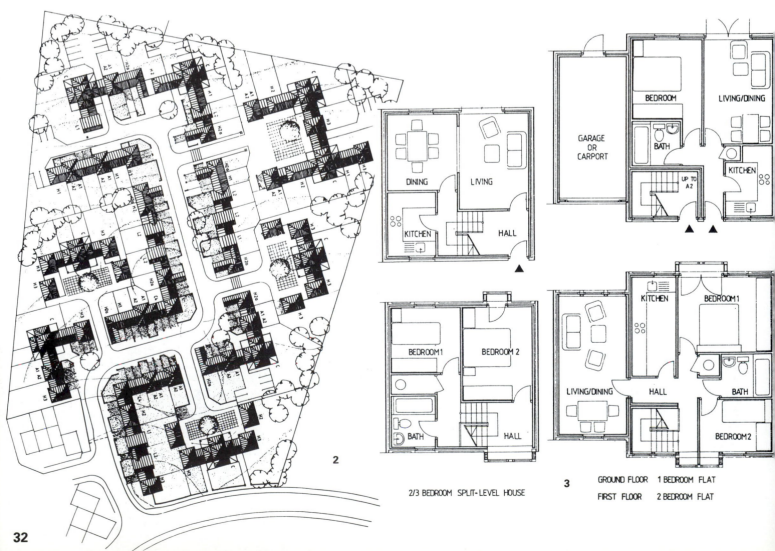

2

2/3 BEDROOM SPLIT-LEVEL HOUSE

3   GROUND FLOOR   1 BEDROOM FLAT
    FIRST FLOOR   2 BEDROOM FLAT

# HOUSING FOR THE ELDERLY · WOKINGHAM · BERKSHIRE

## PHIPPEN RANDALL AND PARKES

1

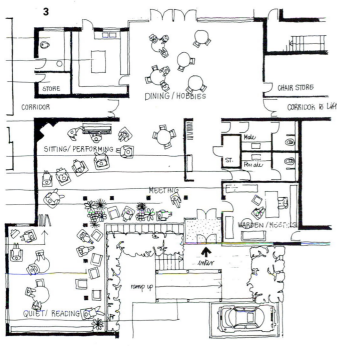

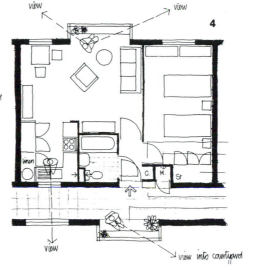

2

3

4

**1** View from garden
**2** Circulation area
**3** Communal area
**4** Typical flat plan
**5** General layout

5

This scheme of 44 self-contained flats is in two storeys to fit naturally into a locality dominated by the existing domestic buildings. The new building is designed to preserve and exploit the mature trees on the site and to incorporate a pleasant Victorian school house as wardens' accommodation. Internally, long straight corridors are avoided and the circulation spaces are made pleasant and interesting by providing views out and giving identity and scope for personalization of flat entrances. The communal areas are immediately adjoining and integrated with the main entrance to encourage their use, but also allowing tenants to retain a sense of independence through the use of secondary entrances.

Built in 1985.

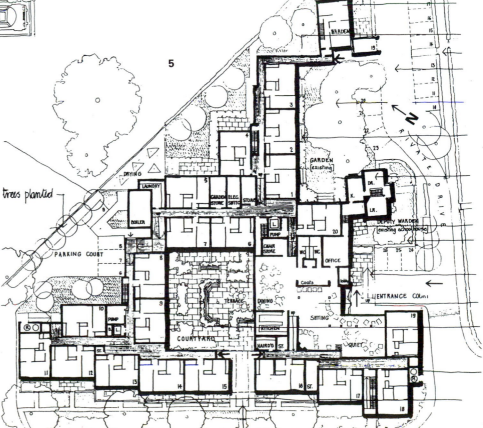

# TENEMENT HOUSING · MARYHILL · GLASGOW
## McGURN LOGAN DUNCAN & OPFER

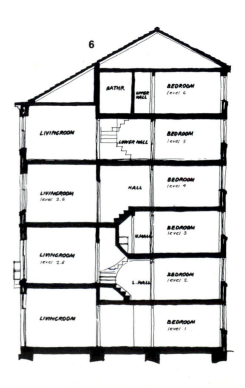

From this Glasgow Housing Association's view of the tenement as a paradigm of medium-rise high-density living, the design concept adopted the traditional Glasgow tenement form of a linear living wall, with formal front and private rear elevations.

A cross-section was developed which married a four-storey front to a six-storey rear, giving traditional-height living rooms to the front, with building-regulation-height bedrooms and kitchens to the rear, and allowed a vertical mix of maisonettes and flats, accessed from a common close.

Built in 1989.

1 View from the shopping centre
2 Typical elevation
3 Aerial view looking south
4 A typical flat plan
5 Site plan
6 Section

# URBAN HOUSING • CRACOW • POLAND
## ARCHITEKTURBÜRO BOLLES-WILSON

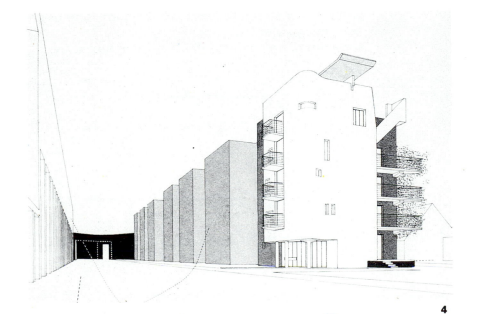

1

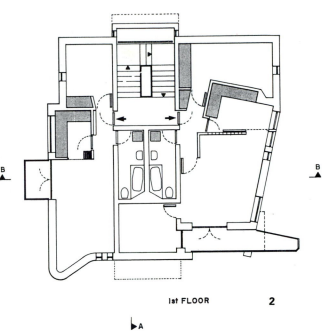

1st FLOOR      2

►A

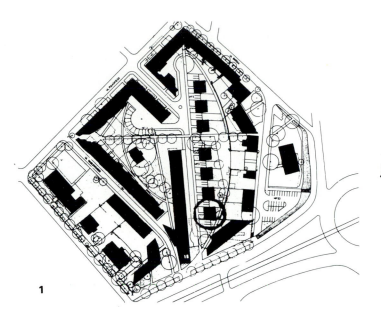

►A    SOUTH ELEVATION    1,100

3

Debniki is an old settlement in Cracow, on the bend of the River Vistula, opposite Wawel castle. It is today a sleepy and neglected housing district.

Inspired by the example of Berlin, local architect Romuald Loegler has produced a master plan for its revitalization and invited a few Polish architects and a few enterprising foreign ones to design a building there.

Peter Wilson's contribution is the design of the first of a row of seven-point blocks of flats which accept the Polish urban flat-dwelling tradition. He has, however, interpreted that tradition in a very personal British way and has designed both plan and elevation with imagination and wit. The elevations in particular eloquently speak Wilson's language. Designed in 1990.

**1** Romuald Loegler's master plan
**2** Typical floor plan
**3** Street perspective
**4** South elevation

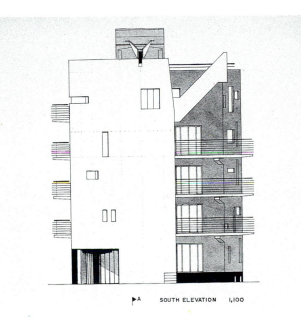

4

# TOLLYMORE TEAHOUSE • COUNTY DOWN • NORTHERN IRELAND
## IAN CAMPBELL & PARTNERS

1

2

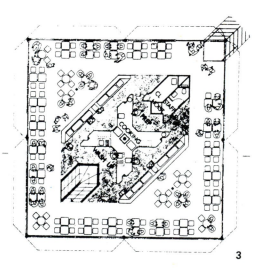

3

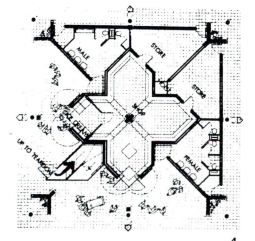

4

The overriding impression of the teahouse is of a building 'that is unique and joyful – redolent with visual reminders of youth and childhood, skilfully sited and confidently detailed.

The teahouse was built in 1981.

Writing in the *Architects' Journal* (July 1981) David Embling described the Tollymore Teahouse which stands in a superb forest park and arboretum on the northern foothills of the Mourne mountains, like this:

**'The plan of the building is square, but two devices are used which give the illusion of more complex geometry – the square is placed diagonally against the strong line of the retaining wall, and the truncated pyramid of the roof is cut away at each corner and at midpoint along each side. Closer approach to the bridge not only reveals the sign "TEAHOUSE" but makes an introduction to what the architect, Ian Campbell, calls his "boy scout construction" – timber poles bolted together and braced with straining wires. Stout round pine posts and triangulated pole-bracing clamp the superstructure and roof into the treed landscape.'**

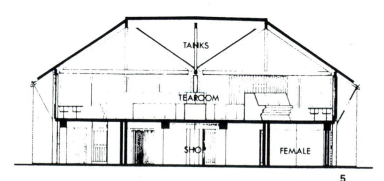

5

1 General view
2 First-floor interior
3 First-floor plan
4 Ground-floor plan
5 Section

# GLOBE THEATRE • SOUTHWARK • LONDON
## THEO CROSBY OF PENTAGRAM

1

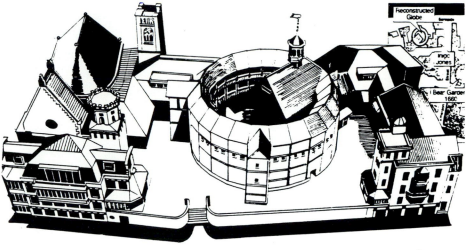

2

3

## PIAZZA LEVEL PLAN

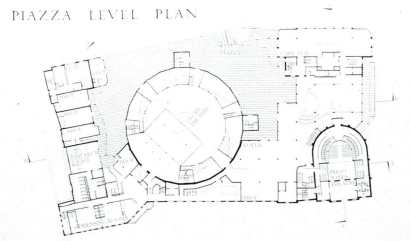

4

5

The Globe theatre will be the focal point of a leisure centre dedicated to the performance of Shakespearian and contemporary theatrical works. It is built on a Thames-side site opposite St Paul's cathedral and close to the site of the original theatre, where most of Shakespeare's plays were first performed, which burned down in 1613.

The design of the theatre follows very closely that of the original one and results from intensive research on the part of the architect, and patient determination on the part of the actor Sam Wanamaker whose brain-child it is.

1  16th-century engraving of the theatre
2  Sketch of the buildings from the river
3  Site plan
4  Plan at piazza level
5  Two sections

# BUILDING SOCIETY HEADQUARTERS • BEXLEYHEATH • KENT

## BROADWAY MALYAN

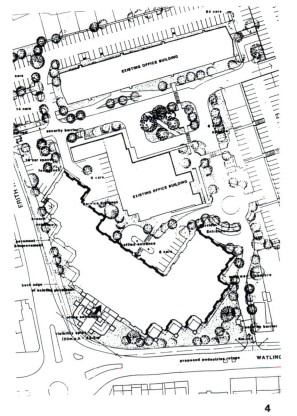

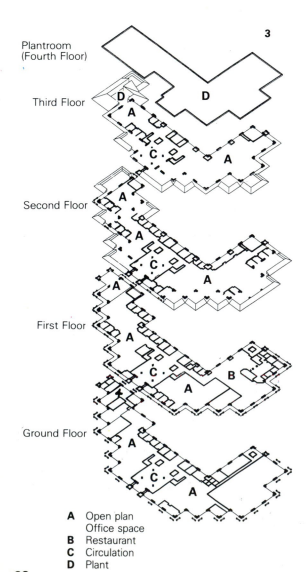

Plantroom
(Fourth Floor)

Third Floor

Second Floor

First Floor

Ground Floor

**A** Open plan
    Office space
**B** Restaurant
**C** Circulation
**D** Plant

Traditional materials (stock bricks, clay roof tiles, lead panelling) are here used with imagination to create a building with a strong, traditionally English character. The building is placed diagonally on the site so as to face the traffic roundabout.

Built in 1989 for the Woolwich Building Society.

1 General view
2 Central entrance lobby
3 Floor plans
4 Site plan

# TOWN END HOUSE · HAVANT · HAMPSHIRE

## MacCORMAC JAMIESON PRICHARD

Here is a fine example of successful spatial planning. There are three kinds of space: a range of cellular offices; an administrative core; and publicly accessible reception and interview rooms. This spatial quality dominates the design, both internally and externally, and — with ingenuity, attention to detail and the use of brick, pitched roof and well-proportioned windows — reinterprets the Hampshire vernacular.

Built in 1989 for Hampshire County Council.

1 View from garden
2 Dominant roof glazing
3 Social services 'clerical hall'
4 Site plan

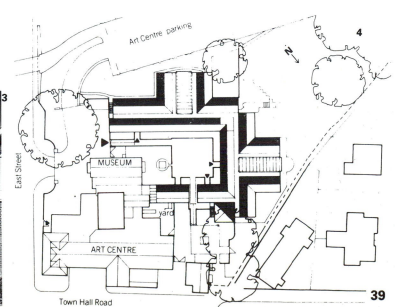

# HQ OFFICE BUILDING • HEMEL HEMPSTEAD • HERTFORDSHIRE
## RENTON HOWARD WOOD LEVIN

1

2

This is BP Oil UK Limited headquarters building at Hemel Hempstead. The architects have carefully designed a large office building to blend satisfactorily with a subtle sloping Chilterns landscape. The office accommodation is grouped at each side of a continuous atrium in a four-storey L-shaped building connected by a covered way to a smaller cafeteria block. The very large car parking area is carefully screened by tree planting.

Built in 1988.

1 View from the south
2 Atrium
3 Site plan
4 Section
5 Plan

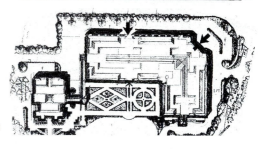

3

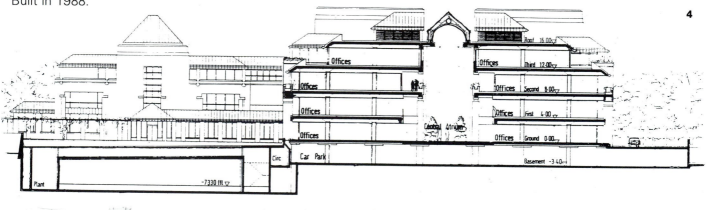

4

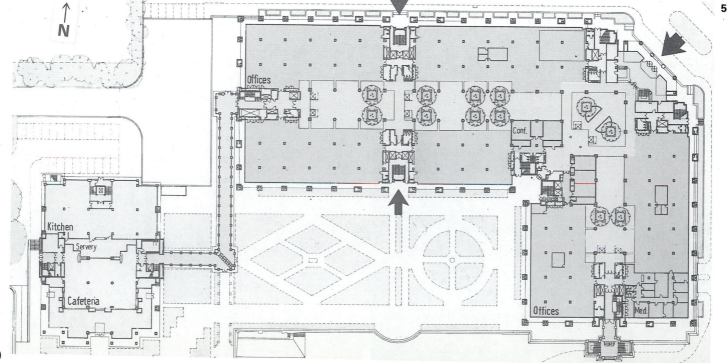

5

# 3
# POST-MODERN

Post-modernism is surely on the way out. It came in at a time when modern architecture was synonymous, in the eyes of the public, with young families being forced to live in tall blocks of flats on huge barrack-like suburban housing estates, with leaking roofs and condensation, with grey concrete walls and high-level walkways. It had many godfathers: pop art and pop music, Disneyland, the environmental and anti-pollution movements, solar energy and energy conservation, community architecture, the adaptation of old buildings to new uses, public participation in planning, a renewed interest in human scale and anthropology. For a time it introduced to architecture colour and decoration and a human scale to which human families could relate. Sometimes it even suggested that architecture could be fun. Its inspiration was, I think, the work of the Spanish architect Antonio Gaudi, around the turn of the century. The winding twisting road which Gaudi followed led away from modern architecture's international style towards an exciting world of fantasy, emotion and irrationality. His work filled the vacuum created by Le Corbusier's Calvinistic logic and Mies' cold classicism. He satisfied people's yearning for richness, decoration and mystery, and he appealed to their sense of fun.

Here in Britain there will always be room for a Gaudiesque figure (Terry Farrell perhaps?) but the work of our post-modernists can't compete with the basic integrity and emotive power of the Spanish master, and post-modernism is already being regarded as a fashion — pastiche-ridden and frivolous without the essential qualities needed for any kind of permanence. People are getting tired of it and it will fade away — like the charleston and the crinoline.

'You say "I'm going to be nice" and then it just isn't possible. The old houses in Britain are being replaced by a toy-town, sugar-candy heaven. What have we done to deserve such architecture?'

**Brian Clarke (BBC Design Awards jury)**

Flats in Barcelona by Antonio Gaudi

# EMBANKMENT PLACE • CHARING CROSS • LONDON
## TERRY FARRELL & COMPANY (Architects) • OVE ARUP & PARTNERS (Engineers)

A dramatic 'air-rights' building constructed above the 120-year-old Charing Cross station, responding to the scale of the adjacent Thames-side buildings. The 13 floors of office space are supported on 18 huge columns which rise through the station platforms to support a series of trussed arches from which the building is suspended – reminiscent of the shape of the original Victorian station roof. The original station forecourt is restored, adjacent streets are pedestrianized and arcaded and Inigo Jones' 17th-century York Watergate restored to its full splendour.

Within the cavernous Victorian arches are a rebuilt theatre, shops, a market and several restaurants.

Built 1989–90.

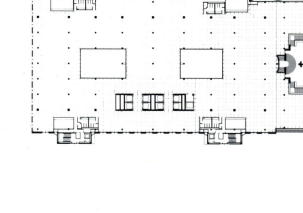

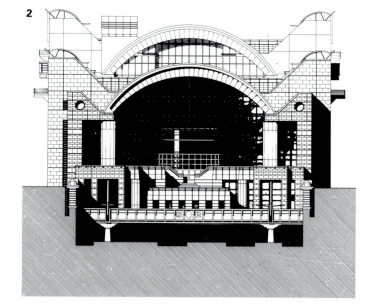

1 View from Embankment Gardens
2 Elevation to River Thames
3 Upper-level plan
4 Diagram of structure
5 Longitudinal section

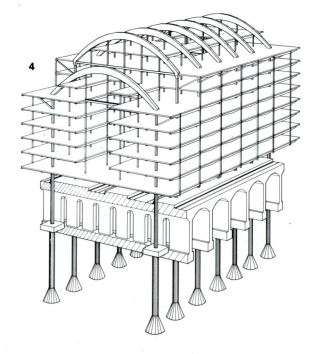

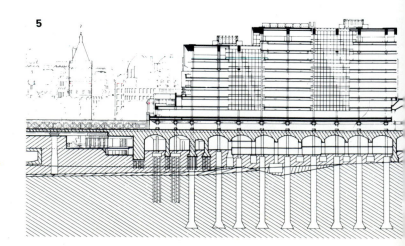

42

# HENLEY REGATTA BUILDING · BERKSHIRE
## TERRY FARRELL & COMPANY

1

2

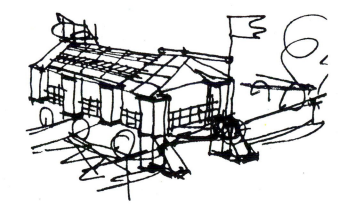

3

Built in 1985, this is a headquarters building for the Henley Royal Regatta. It is really a clubroom and a boat-store.

**'A bold design striking a harmonious chord on a sensitive site next to the bridge (over the Thames). The Venetian window offers a magnetic view over the river.'**

1 Elevation to the River Thames
2 View from the river
3 Clubroom
4 Architect's sketches

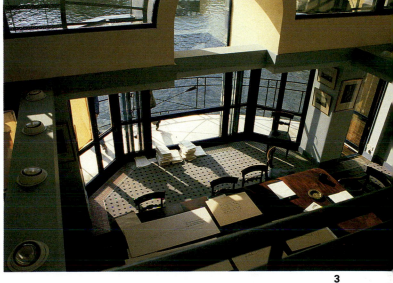

4

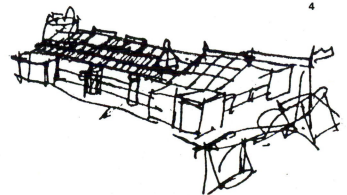

# JENCKS' FAMILY HOUSE • BAYSWATER • LONDON

## CHARLES JENCKS AND TERRY FARRELL

This 19th-century house has been extensively remodelled – externally, with new rooftop study and garden conservatories, and, internally, a centrally located staircase which acts as the focus of movement throughout the house and is cut at various points to give surprising cross-views. The new timber roof was designed in a complex spatial manner. The conservatories link the interior spaces with terrace and garden.

A fascinating house – full of interesting vistas and complex symbolism – built 1979–81.

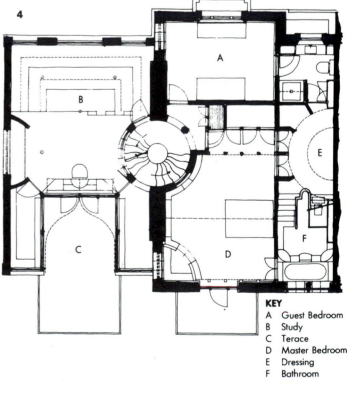

**KEY**
A  Cloaks
B  Reception
C  Utility
D  Kitchen
E  Dining Room
F  Living Room
G  Study
H  Conservatory
J  Garden Stairs

**KEY**
A  Guest Bedroom
B  Study
C  Terrace
D  Master Bedroom
E  Dressing
F  Bathroom

1  Central staircase
2  Exterior
3  Ground-floor plan
4  First-floor plan

# A 'LIVE–WORK' CONCEPT • CAMDEN • NORTH LONDON
## JESTICO & WHILES

An inner-city experiment in north London, on an awkward triangular site, where the architects have designed two related buildings with workshops on the ground and first floors and residential accommodation on the second and third. Each type of user has its own set of stairs and lifts – well separated from one another. All flats have terraces and balconies and are entered from an upper-level street. The 'live–work' concept is strongly expressed elevationally and underlined by the use of alternative bands of brickwork.

Built in 1986.

1 General view
2 Upper-level street
3 Second-floor plan
4 Site plan
5 Section

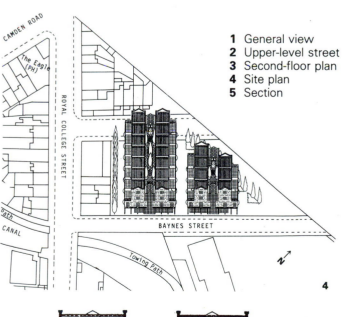

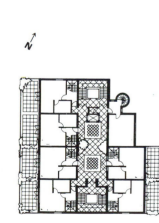

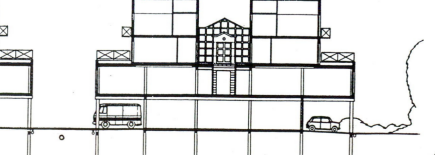

# HORSELYDOWN SQUARE • BERMONDSEY • LONDON
## WICKHAM & ASSOCIATES

1

Julyan Wickham has here demonstrated his passionate belief in the enduring values of urban architecture. Very close to Tower Bridge on the River Thames he has created two urban squares — each different in character — surrounded by high-density buildings containing shops and offices on the two lowest floors, with flats above. The squares are separated by a tall, very narrow street reminiscent of the alley-ways of old London docklands. Flats are reached from an 'interior street', with the end ones three storeys high, with terraces and turrets emerging through the roof; the turrets mark the entrance to the main square.

Built in 1989.

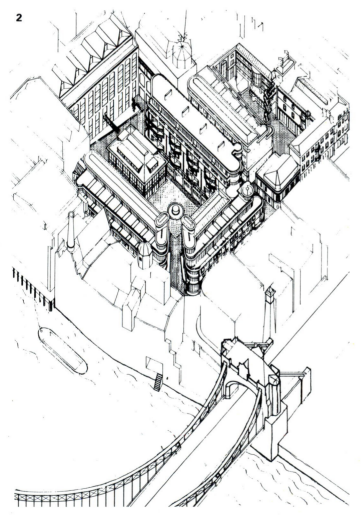

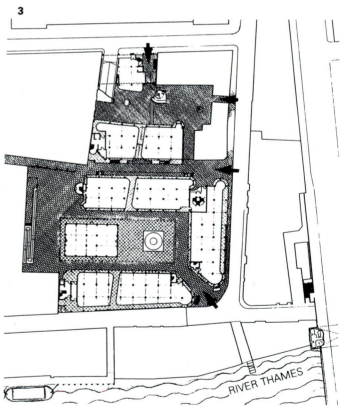

RIVER THAMES

1 General view
2 Axonometric view from Tower Bridge
3 Layout plan

# FLATS IN BERMONDSEY • LONDON DOCKLANDS

## CAMPBELL ZOGOLOVITCH WILKINSON GOUGH

Writing in 1989 in the *Architectural Review* Frances Anderton called this building 'a ray of sunshine on a gloomy London dockland'. Certainly this dreary stretch of the River Thames needed a colourful, stimulating and mildly fantastic building. The architects have given it just that, with the river elevation painted a bright red.

The building provides 17 two-storey flats, designed in scissors fashion so that all the open-plan living rooms face the river, with large balconies and fabulous framed views both upstream and downstream. Bedroom window walls are scalloped so as to twist the window towards the sun and avoid overlooking by neighbours. Built in 1988, the building has a reinforced concrete frame and projects partly into the river.

**1** Elevation to River
   Thames
**2** Typical flat plan
**3** Section

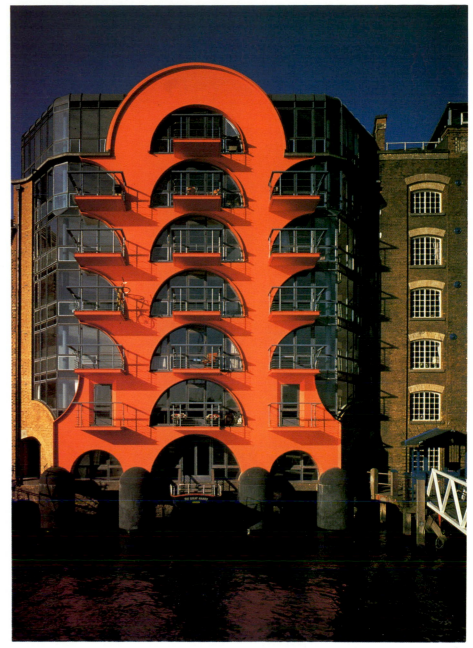

1

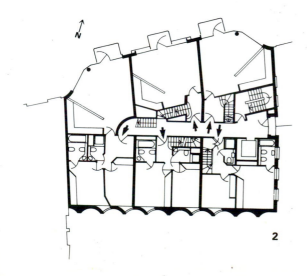

2

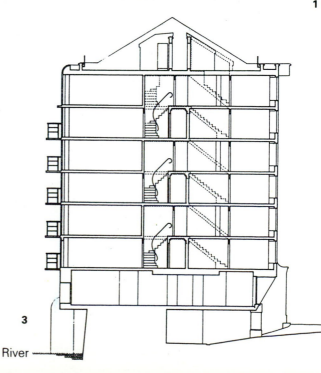

3

River →

# CAUSEWAYSIDE LIBRARY • EDINBURGH

## ANDREW MERRYLEES

This interesting library is located in one of Edinburgh's inner housing areas – among row-houses and hotels. The planning principle was to place all ancillary accommodation on the perimeter of a major rectangular space, so as to create an uninterrupted internal usable area. The general ambience of this area, at each floor level, is warm and restful. The external fully glazed staircase towers are strong decorative elements in the architectural composition. The 900 mm planning module of the interior is repeated in the fenestration, lying like a net over the building. Lift towers and walls are faced with Scottish limestone.

Built in 1987.

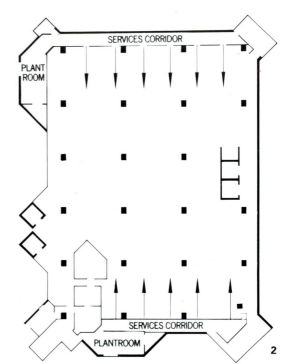

1 Entrance
elevation
2 Typical floor
plan
3 Typical reading
room

# 4
# CLASSICAL REVIVAL

All through the Modern Movement era in Britain there were a few architects – notably Raymond Erith – who refused to accept the principles of the Athens Charter and were unimpressed by the teaching of Walter Gropius, Le Corbusier or Mies van der Rohe. They regarded the advent of the Movement as a major international tragedy. They thought of themselves as Renaissance men. They studied ancient Greece and Rome, the Orders of Architecture and the writings of Vitruvius and Palladio. Some of them spent their summer holidays in Greece and Italy and came back with detailed sketches of the Parthenon, the Colosseum and the island of Miletus.

Today Quinlan Terry (who grew up in Erith's office), Robert Adam III of the Winchester Design Group, Leon Krier and John Simpson are busy designing imposing façades recalling Palladio at first glance, but often using inferior materials and sometimes poor detailing and without his genius for creating convincing sculptural form and aesthetic excitement. For Ictinus and Callicrates and for Palladio plan, elevation and use of material were all talking the same architectural language – with remarkable eloquence.

Walk behind Terry's imposing neo-Classical façades facing the River Thames at Richmond and you will find a modern office layout almost identical to those built all over Britain in the 1960s and 1970s (and elsewhere), most of them with glass-and-aluminium curtain-wall elevations. Visit Adam's computer centre in Hampshire and you will find the latest models of sophisticated computers hiding behind neo-Palladian brick-and-stone walls adorned with Corinthian columns. Adam has used the same neo-Palladian style in designing a new office block 30 storeys high.

The proposed redevelopment of two very large London sites – at Spitalfields and Paternoster Square (just north of St Paul's) – has given our neo-Classicists an opportunity to develop their ideas. The suggested layouts of both sites have a strong Beaux-Arts look to them, with a rather rigid formality very different from the mediaeval street pattern which Londoners know so well. It is to be hoped that the rigid formality and inflexibility of the Beaux-Arts tradition can be reinterpreted satisfactorily to incorporate the unforeseen needs of future Londoners.

Bernini's colonnade, Rome

A look at Canary Wharf in Docklands which also has a strong Beaux-Arts layout does not give us much hope that this will happen; these buildings are situated in an 'enterprise zone' – created by the Government to encourage developers to develop there – where planning permission is not required. As I watch the Canary Wharf buildings lift their unwelcome bulk above the London skyline I am reminded of one of the Athens Charter's precepts: 'Architecture detached from the serious social problems of its time is not good architecture'.

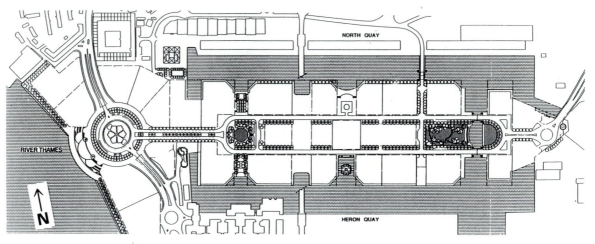

Canary Wharf, London Docklands

# SAINSBURY WING • NATIONAL GALLERY • LONDON
## VENTURI, SCOTT BROWN & ASSOCIATES

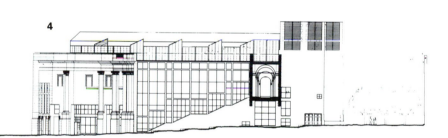

1

2

3

4

Built on an awkwardly shaped site on the corner of Trafalgar Square, the 'Sainsbury Wing' houses one of the world's foremost collections of early Italian and northern Renaissance paintings. Stylistically, the wing is designed to relate to the original building (designed in 1838 by William Wilkins) while maintaining its own identity as a work of contemporary architecture. It is built of the same Portland stone and observes the cornice height of the National Gallery. The Wilkins columns and pilasters are exactly reproduced as decoration on the curved elevation of the new building in what the architects call 'innovative and unexpected ways'. The main galleries are placed on the third floor, approached by a splendid processional staircase from the entrance foyer. The lower floors contain temporary galleries, lecture theatre, shop, restaurant and conference rooms.

The gallery was opened in 1991.

1 General view
2 Link between the two galleries
3 Venturi's sketch of the galleries
4 East elevation
5 Site plan

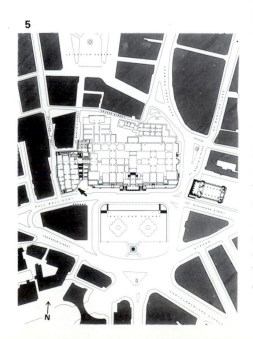

5

# PAVILION IN PRINCES STREET GARDENS • EDINBURGH
## ALLIES & MORRISON

1

Allies and Morrison's welcome pavilion in Edinburgh's central park. A simple and elegant contemporary interpretation of Classical architecture, this little pavilion fits unobtrusively into the urban elegance of the park. Columns are of Scottish granite and roof of Scottish slate.

Built in 1988.

2

# COMPUTER CENTRE • DOGMERSFIELD PARK • HAMPSHIRE
## ROBERT ADAM OF WINCHESTER DESIGN ARCHITECTS

**1**

Robert Adam describes his computer centre at Dogmersfield Park thus:

**'The new extension is classical but distinctly modern and has a generic rather than subservient relationship to the original Georgian house.'**

It is particularly noticeable that the elevations do not very convincingly express the open plan of the interior.
Built in 1985.

**1** General view from the west
**2** Site plan

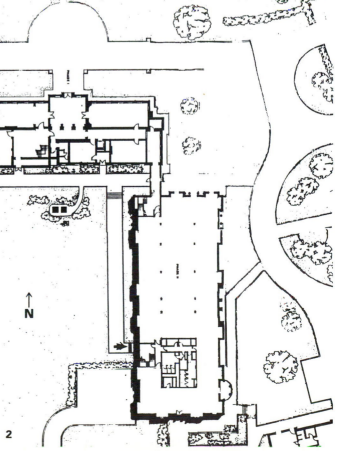

N

**2**

# HOUSING IN VENICE

## JAMES GOWAN

The Venice housing authority IACP invited a few well-known European architects to design a high-density housing scheme on a Venetian island which would 'fuse modern architecture and Venetian urbanism'. James Gowan responded with a formal neo-Palladian layout of four-storey flats in two groups, each overlooking a central court, the architecture responding to 'the elementary and functional nature of classicism, rather than its theatricality'. Small workshops for artisans are packed into the ground floor, with a few shops. Detached stairways give separate access to the flats.

Designed in 1985.

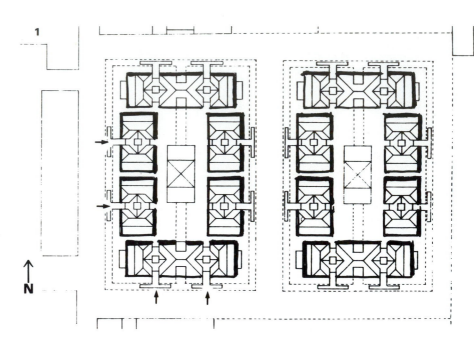

1 Site plan
2 Flat plans, typical elevation and cross-section

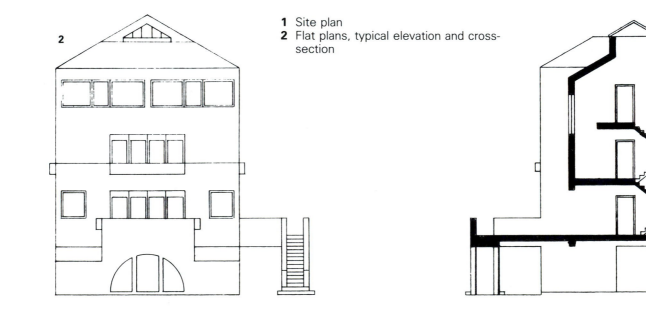

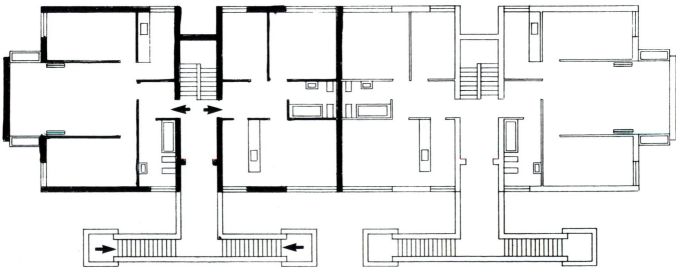

# STUDENTS' RESTAURANT AND COMMON ROOM • SIXTH-FORM COLLEGE • WALTHAM FOREST • LONDON

## VAN HEYNINGEN & HAWARD

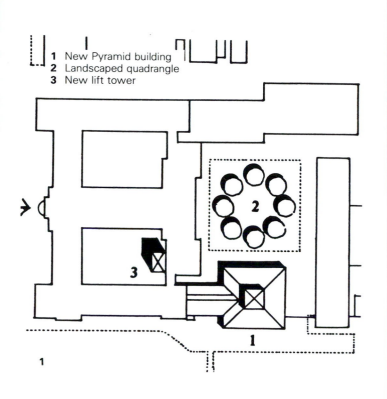

1 New Pyramid building
2 Landscaped quadrangle
3 New lift tower

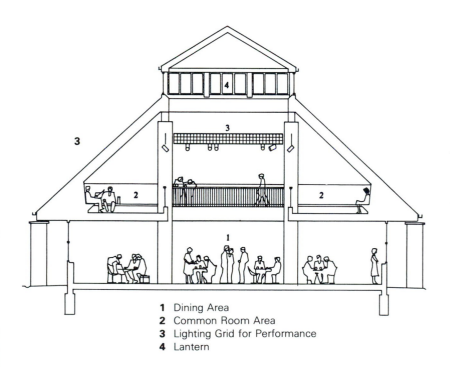

1 Dining Area
2 Common Room Area
3 Lighting Grid for Performance
4 Lantern

Here is modern, restrained Classicism at its best. The architects have demolished an existing awkwardly situated building and added a new one skilfully located so as to form a new landscaped quadrangle. The ground-floor restaurant is entered from the main school building and is surrounded by a formal loggia. Its central area rises three floors to a large roof-light and is overlooked by the first-floor common room which is in fact a series of balconies – also entered directly from the main school building.

The simple formal symmetrical composition is eloquent and impressive.

Built in 1990.

1 Site plan
2 Interior
3 Section

# PATERNOSTER SQUARE REDEVELOPMENT • CITY OF LONDON
## ARCHITECTS: ARUP ASSOCIATES and JOHN SIMPSON

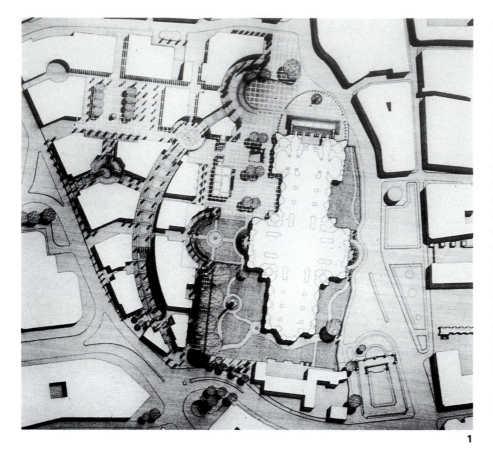

**1**

Two proposals by Arup Associates and John Simpson for a 7-acre (2.8 ha) site just north of St Paul's cathedral. The Simpson scheme is preferred by the Prince of Wales.

The entire Arup scheme at ground level is pedestrianized. Vehicular access to all buildings is from an undergound service basement. A new Cathedral Close creates a wide varied public 'surround' for St Paul's, with a new piazza at the western end, a quiet contemplation garden and colonnaded south terrace. A curved shopping arcade will create a new pedestrian route linking Cheapside with Ludgate Hill. It will also have direct access to St Paul's Underground station. The scheme allows for a landscaped market square with fine views towards the cathedral.

The original Simpson scheme proposed a street network which was a fairly logical extension of the surrounding area.

During the late 1980s both proposals were shown at several major exhibitions and discussed at length by the media. In the early 1990s the Arup scheme was withdrawn and – in close collaboration with Terry Farrell and the American classicist Thomas Beeby – the Simpson layout was altered, creating a series of island buildings, each of which would be designed by a different architect – in a neo-Classical manner. Simpson's new colonnaded Paternoster Square was given a more central location, with most of the 'modern' mediaeval streets leading in to it.

**2**

56

# RICHMOND-ON-THAMES RIVERSIDE DEVELOPMENT • SURREY

## ERITH & TERRY

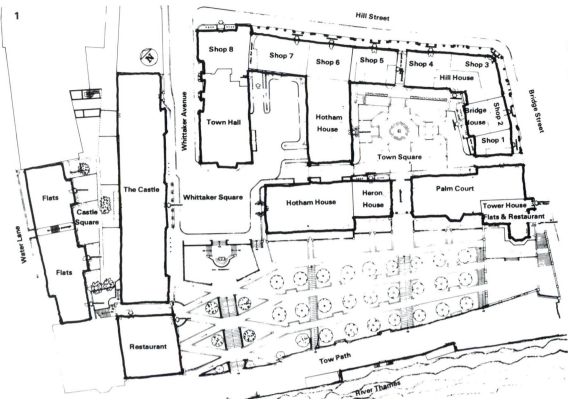

1

**1** Site layout
**2** General view of Town Square
**3** Detail view of Town Square: the concrete raft of the underground car park is cleverly concealed under the cobbled surface.

2

3

A major redevelopment of part of Richmond's riverfront, illustrating the architect's four 'revolutionary' principles: load-bearing brick walls, pitched slate roofs, sash windows and a basic 40-ft (12 m) span.

Offices, flats, shops and two restaurants are grouped to form several urban squares.

The elevations remind us of the 17th rather than the 20th century. Here is perhaps a good example of architectural façadism: look behind Terry's neo-Palladian façades and you will find a very large open office space, a modern flat or a restaurant.

Built 1985–88.

# SPITALFIELDS REDEVELOPMENT • EAST LONDON

## FIVE PROPOSALS

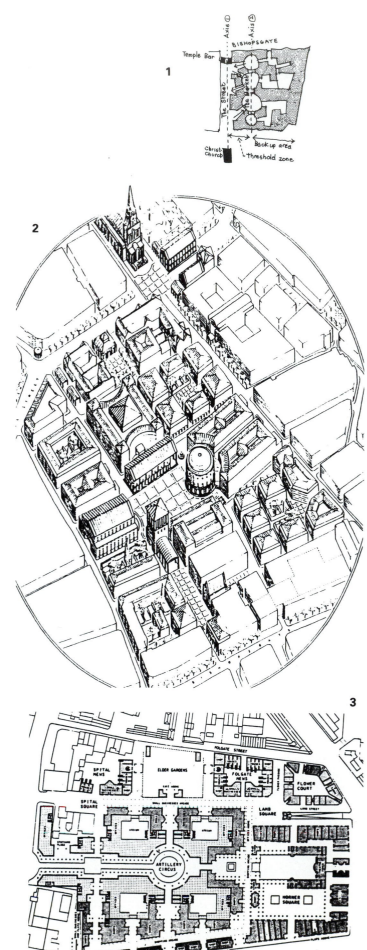

When the Spitalfields market moved out of east London a very large site (dominated by Hawksmoor's fine Christchurch) became available for development as offices, shops and housing. Competing developers invited a number of well-known architects to suggest how this could best be done. Leon Krier, Quinlan Terry, MacCormac Jamieson Prichard and Swanke Hayden Connell have all submitted proposals.

The first master plan to be published was by Leon Krier who proposed a network of narrow streets, with squares, crescents and internal courts, and formal Classical architecture. MacCormac Jamieson Prichard's scheme had a stronger impact and won support from the local cosmopolitan population. With a formal Beaux-Arts layout it suggested a series of internal arcaded shopping streets and grouped office buildings in the centre of the site, with smaller buildings on the perimeter.

It is indeed tragic that the MacCormac scheme has apparently been superseded by another designed by the American architects Swanke Hayden Connell which has a similar Beaux-Arts layout but lacks the sensitivity and appropriateness of the MacCormac proposals which incorporated the developers' requirements for large office buildings without sacrificing the vitality of the street.

1 Gordon Cullen suggested a desirable form for any future development
2 Leon Krier's very Classical proposals
3 MacCormac Jamieson Prichard's Beaux-Arts layout
4 One of MacCormac's internal arcaded streets

# CANARY WHARF OFFICE DEVELOPMENT • LONDON DOCKLANDS

## I.M. PEI, SKIDMORE OWINGS MERRILL & CESAR PELLI

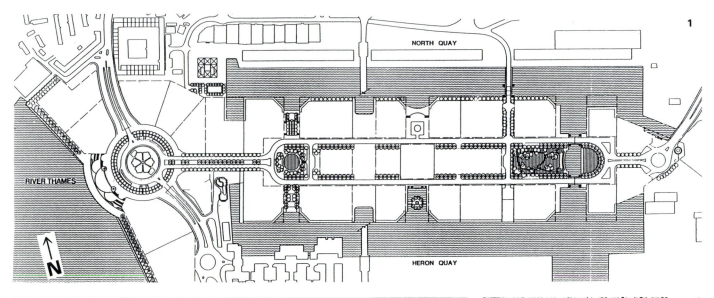

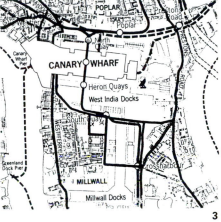

What can one say about Canary Wharf? An enormous high-density office complex, it satisfies the modern commercial organization's demand for lofty open office space and the desirable 'proximity' of office staff, and it includes the tallest building in Europe – Cesar Pelli's 850-ft (260 m) office tower. As one critic has said: 'It would look much more at home in Chicago or Houston than in London town'; and this critic has written about it in the introduction to this chapter: 'As I watch the Canary Wharf buildings lift their unwelcome bulk above the London skyline I am reminded of one of the Athens Charter's precepts: "Architecture detached from the serious social problems of its time is not good architecture".'

The Canary Wharf development solves none of east London's problems – except to give employment to local people – and it totally ignores its neighbours.

1 Layout plan
2 The well-landscaped central area
3 Location plan
4 Aerial view, looking towards the Thames

# 5
# HI-TECH

Undoubtedly here to stay; Paxton, Foster, Arup and Grimshaw have made sure of that.

In the mediaeval era some critics thought that their master masons were going too far in building the Gothic cathedral. With its great height, its flying buttresses and its enormous stained-glass windows it was the hi-tech building of its time. The critics said it would fall down. And some did. But most of them stayed up for a thousand years and – magnificently – are still with us today.

The recent work of Arups, Foster, Rogers, Grimshaw and Hopkins is impressive. Their understanding of structure is impressive, and the way they use it to create cathedral-like spaces for dealing in shares and banking, for sport and recreation, shows the way forward. And if one day we start going to church again in large numbers, the same understanding of structure and the same love of reinforced concrete, steel, aluminium, glass and plastics will enable the next generation of architects to create modern cathedrals three or four times the size of Canterbury or Wells.

Who can doubt that, as we move into the 21st century, this impressive harnessing of modern technology, with the honesty of expression which usually accompanies it, will continue to solve the specific and constantly changing problems of the day?

Before the end of this century we will almost certainly see three interesting illustrations of this trend – two of them at Heathrow Airport: Rogers' £800 million terminal five and Grimshaw's British Airways operation control building; and one in Hong Kong: Foster's huge new airport terminal (echoing the structural excitement of his Stansted Airport).

And high technology will no doubt develop hand-in-hand with flexibility and demountability, as the ways in which we do things change and the cost of adapting old buildings to new unforeseen uses increases.

The Crystal Palace under construction

# SCHLUMBERGER RESEARCH CENTRE • CAMBRIDGE
## MICHAEL HOPKINS & PARTNERS

**1**

**2**

This is an adventurous prototype building. It serves the oil industry and explores all aspects of drilling, pumping and testing, and provides laboratories, offices, conference hall and restaurants – all housed under one gigantic roof in a single-storey open plan with an average ceiling height of 10 m.

The structure of the building is dramatic. The Teflon-covered roof is suspended by steel cables from tall masts, giving the whole building a tent-like appearance.

Built in 1985.

**1** General view
**2** Interior
**3** Section
**4** Part elevation (opposite)

**3**

# HONG KONG & SHANGHAI BANK

## SIR NORMAN FOSTER AND PARTNERS

One of the 1980s' most interesting buildings – perhaps Sir Norman Foster's greatest achievement. Uncompromisingly hi-tech, with all floors hung from a series of enormous trusses located every eighth floor, it nevertheless slots gracefully and unobtrusively into the high-rise urban concentration of downtown Hong Kong.

1

2

# YACHT HOUSE • THE NEW FOREST • HAMPSHIRE

## RICHARD HORDEN

1

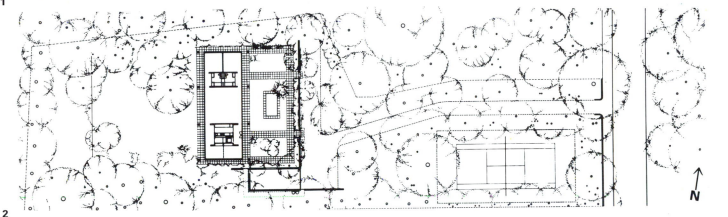

2

3

4

Richard Horden is a keen yachtsman and here he uses standard yacht components for what is really a prototype prefabricated house. Steel, aluminium and neoprene are carefully detailed, in a sophisticated and very precise manner, on a five-by-four grid, to create an elegant house beautifully related to its natural surroundings of pine trees, rhododendron and azalea shrubs. The Hampshire planners didn't like the design of the house but gave it planning permission because, when built, it would be screened from view.

The house was built in 1983.

**1** Entrance elevation
**2** Site plan
**3** Roof plan
**4** Detail of structure

# FARNBOROUGH COLLEGE OF TECHNOLOGY • HAMPSHIRE

## COLIN STANSFIELD SMITH (Hampshire County Architect)

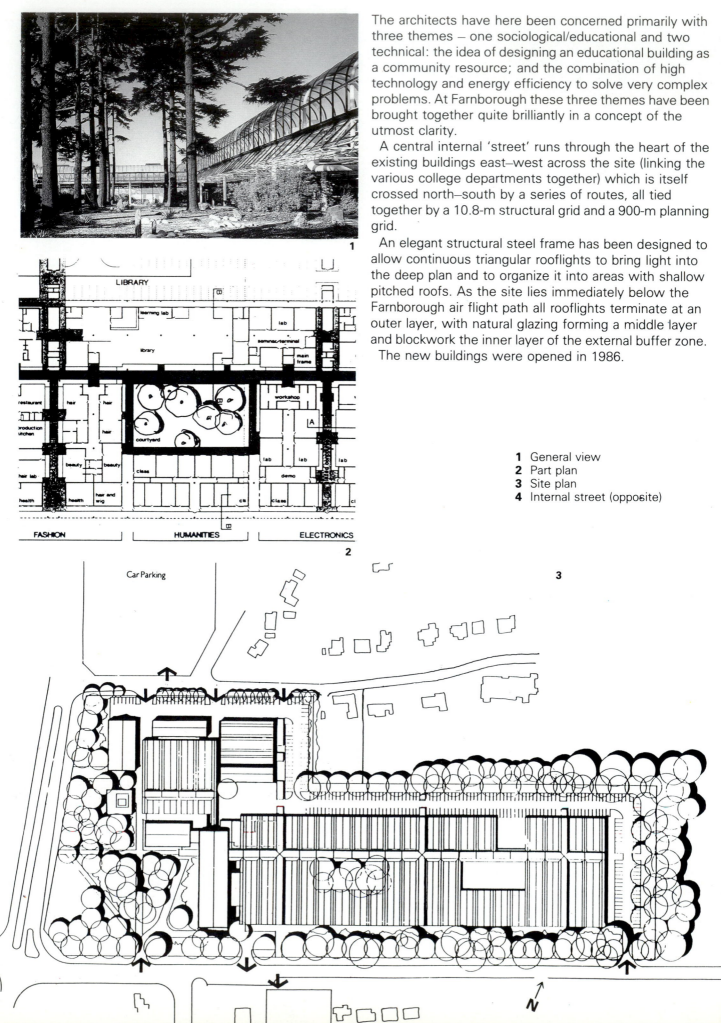

The architects have here been concerned primarily with three themes — one sociological/educational and two technical: the idea of designing an educational building as a community resource; and the combination of high technology and energy efficiency to solve very complex problems. At Farnborough these three themes have been brought together quite brilliantly in a concept of the utmost clarity.

A central internal 'street' runs through the heart of the existing buildings east–west across the site (linking the various college departments together) which is itself crossed north–south by a series of routes, all tied together by a 10.8-m structural grid and a 900-m planning grid.

An elegant structural steel frame has been designed to allow continuous triangular rooflights to bring light into the deep plan and to organize it into areas with shallow pitched roofs. As the site lies immediately below the Farnborough air flight path all rooflights terminate at an outer layer, with natural glazing forming a middle layer and blockwork the inner layer of the external buffer zone.

The new buildings were opened in 1986.

**1** General view
**2** Part plan
**3** Site plan
**4** Internal street (opposite)

# MUSEUM OF THE MOVING IMAGE
## • LONDON
### AVERY ASSOCIATES

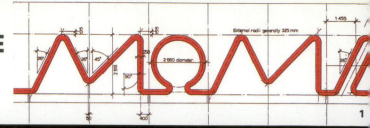

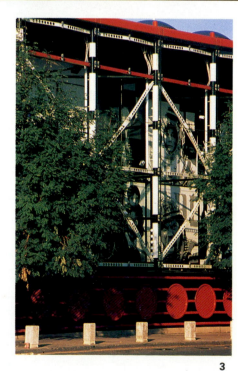

The world's first museum to trace the technological, aesthetic and social development of the moving-image-making process, from the earliest cave paintings to film, television and beyond. Part of London's South Bank arts complex, the museum is – amazingly and very successfully – located underneath Waterloo Bridge on the River Thames. It has a light steel structure and glass walls.

The museum opened in 1989.

**1** MOMI logo
**2** General view
**3** Part elevation
**4** Section

# FLATS AND WORKSHOPS · HAMBURG · GERMANY
## ALSOP & STÖRMER

Built in 1993 — a bold attempt to provide flats and workshops for young families and single people in a run-down area of Hamburg — in a manner acceptable to them.

A structural grid has been used economically and with considerable ingenuity.

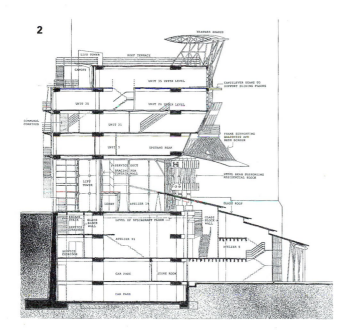

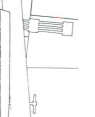

1 Model
2 Section
3 Typical floor plan
4 Elevation

# HAMBURG FERRY TERMINAL • GERMANY
## ALSOP & STÖRMER

A dramatic well-articulated design, with a nautical flavour, for a ferry terminal on the River Elbe in Hamburg. Two buildings connected by a glass bridge. The curved form of the main building echoes the forms of ships and nautical structures.

Precast concrete has been used for both buildings which are raised on legs to prevent damage in the event of flooding and to allow vehicle circulation beneath. The roof is a translucent plastics membrane.

This is the first phase of a three-phase project – built in 1991–93.

1

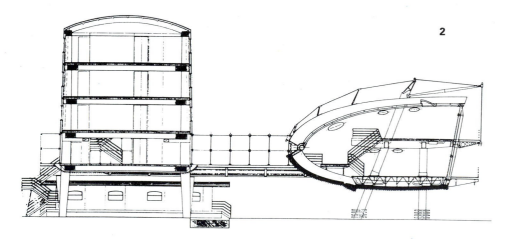

2

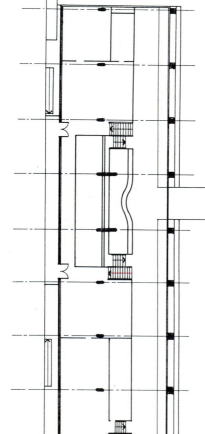

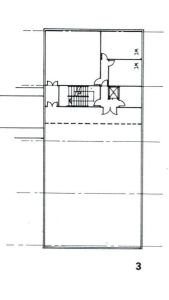

4

3

1 General view (model)
2 Section
3 Plan
4 Larger building under construction (1991)

# RESCUE CONTROL CENTRE • WALSALL • WEST MIDLANDS

## BUILDING DESIGN PARTNERSHIP

**1**  **2**

'A celebration of engineering in metal and glass'. This control centre overlooking the M6 motorway in the English Midlands was designed by BDP for the Royal Automobile Club. It is designed to be eye-catching, with its strong sculptural form and tall masts – seen by motorists travelling at speed – floodlit at night. From the entrance a continuous staircase rises through the building to all floors which are in fact open-plan terraces.

Built in 1989.

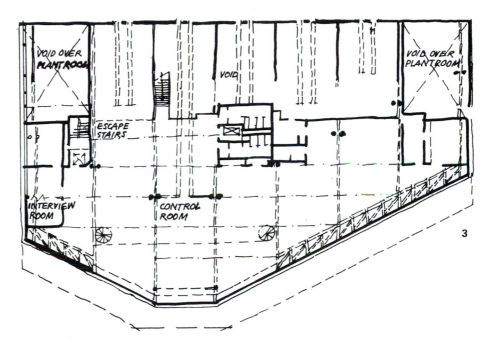

**3**

**1** General view
**2** Interior
**3** Plan at upper level
**4** Section

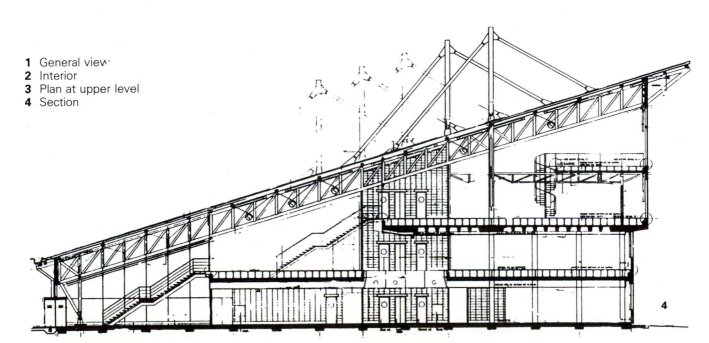

**4**

# FINANCIAL TIMES PRINTING WORKS • LONDON DOCKLANDS
## NICHOLAS GRIMSHAW & PARTNERS

**1**

The Financial Times printing works in London's Docklands is a clear statement of its internal organization. Its two great printing presses are visible to commuters on the A13 through a 96 × 16 m frameless glass structural wall – giving the building the status of a new London landmark.

Built in 1988 the building had to be completed and ready to receive the printing presses within twelve months of the initial briefing session. Within this tight programme a special glazing and structural system was developed, including modelling and testing of full-scale prototypes.

**2**

**1** General view
**2** Structural glass wall
**3** Section

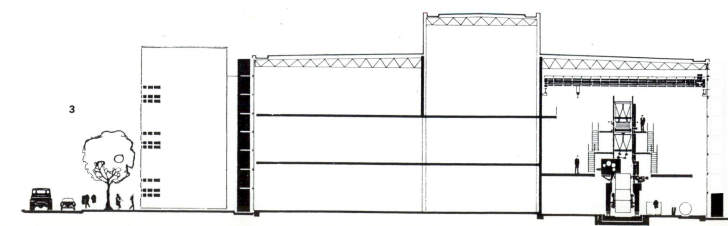

**3**

# RIVER THAMES FLOOD BARRIER • WOOLWICH • SOUTH EAST LONDON

## GLC ARCHITECTS & ENGINEERS (CHIEF ARCHITECT PETER JONES)

1

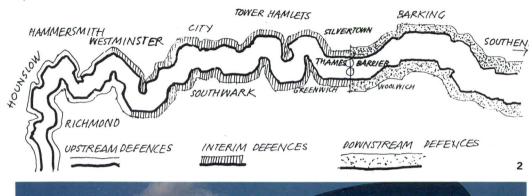

2

For several centuries the River Thames periodically overflowed its banks and caused very serious flooding in London. One of the last projects of the Greater London Council – abolished by the Government in the mid-1980s – was to build a flood barrier at Woolwich which prevents flood water entering the city.

The barrier is in fact a very successful collaboration between architect and engineer – at a cost of almost £500 million.

A series of great D-shaped gates which normally lie on the river bed are lifted into a vertical position hydraulically, creating a solid wall right across the river. The hydraulic machinery is protected by timber-framed steel-tile-covered shell-like structures aerodynamically shaped to counteract the force of the wind which whistles up the river valley.

Built in 1984.

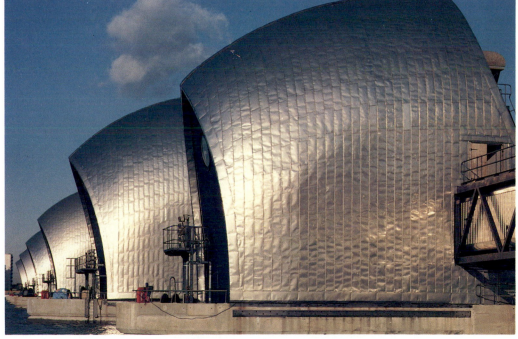

3

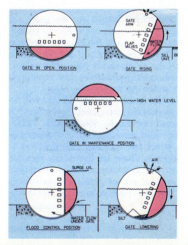

4

1 View from Woolwich
2 London's flood protection scheme
3 General view from the river bank
4 Operation diagram

**2**

**3**

One of the 1980s' few seminal buildings. Sir Richard Rogers' design is basically very simple – a large rectangular atrium space, with a glazed roof, overlooked by open office accommodation designed as galleries. Because all the ancillary accommodation is located along the perimeter of the irregular site the building slots unobtrusively – almost paradoxically – into London's mediaeval street pattern; it never reads as one very large building, but rather as a series of smaller ones, each

relating directly to a very narrow street. Rogers has in fact quite brilliantly resolved the 'unforeseeable growth' dilemma of the Lloyds organization: the essence of his design is an arrangement that will allow for any reasonable growth over the next decade to be accommodated and still maintain the integrity of the single-volume underwriting room.

Built in 1986.

**1** Atrium (opposite)
**2** General view (a painting by Richard Downes)
**3** External stairs
**4** Roof plan

**4**

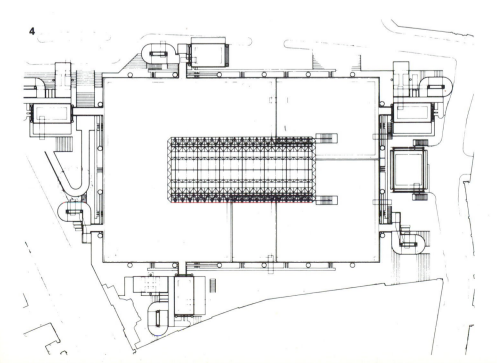

# BRITISH PAVILION at 1992 SEVILLE EXPO • SPAIN
## COMPETITION ENTRY
## SPENCE & WEBSTER

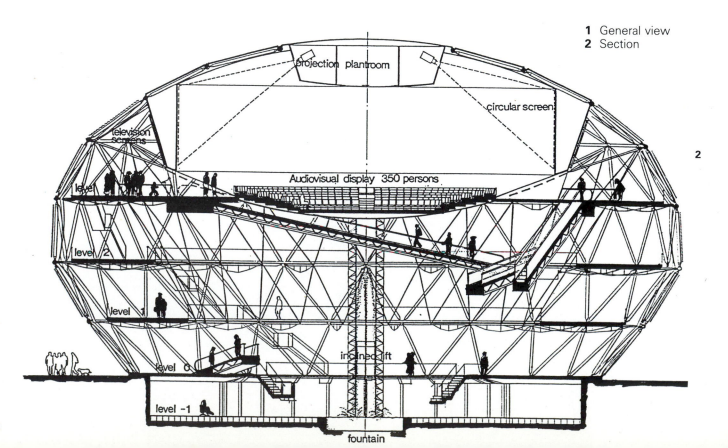

1

One of four recent projects by Spence and Webster illustrating their belief that building technology should 'approach nature' by automatically responding to external conditions and making maximum use of ambient energy. In the case of this competition entry for the British pavilion at the 1992 Seville Expo (won by Nicholas Grimshaw) external automatically adjustable louvres control lighting levels and can also 'perform' to electronically composed music. Cooling is provided partially by heat pumps and mainly by evaporation from internal fountains, trees and fine water-spray diffusers, in combination with the natural updraught.

1  General view
2  Section

# CAMDEN • **LONDON AND** SEVILLE • SPAIN

## NICHOLAS GRIMSHAW & PARTNERS

1

Nicholas Grimshaw's competition-winning design for the British pavilion at the 1992 Seville Expo uses structural glass and solar energy dramatically and with considerable elegance: rooftop solar panels absorb maximum sun and provide energy for a water wall which cools the building. A massive cellular wall protects the building from the late afternoon sun.

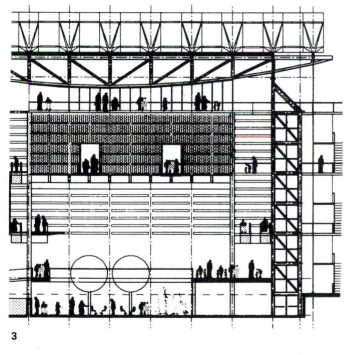

2

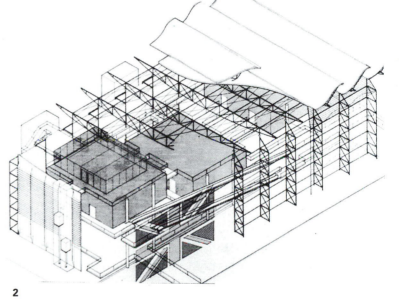

3

Grimshaw at his technological best. Terrace houses on the Grand Union canal – the first truly hi-tech houses to be built in London for many years (1989).

4

# TERMINAL BUILDING • LONDON'S THIRD AIRPORT • STANSTED • ESSEX
## FOSTER ASSOCIATES

The keynote of Sir Norman Foster's design is flexibility — both in planning and in structure — to allow for future unforeseen developments in flying requirements. The passenger accommodation is subdivided by easily demountable lightweight partitions. Umbrella-like tubular steel structural columns are placed on a grid of 36 × 36 m, supporting a lightweight roof. All services are located within the columns and underground.

The building was opened in 1991.

**1** Night view of building
**2** Entrance elevation
**3** Location plan
**4** Diagrammatic floor plan
**5** Roof structure
**6** Concourse interior
**7** Diagrammatic section

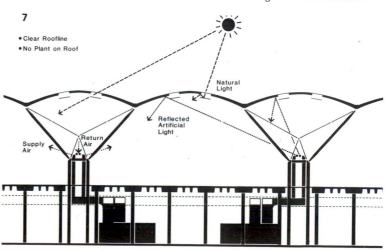

- Clear Roofline
- No Plant on Roof

Natural Light

Reflected Artificial Light

Supply Air

Return Air

- Floor Mounted Plant
- Easy Access

# GATWICK AIRPORT · NORTH TERMINAL

YRM PARTNERSHIP

1

2

**3**

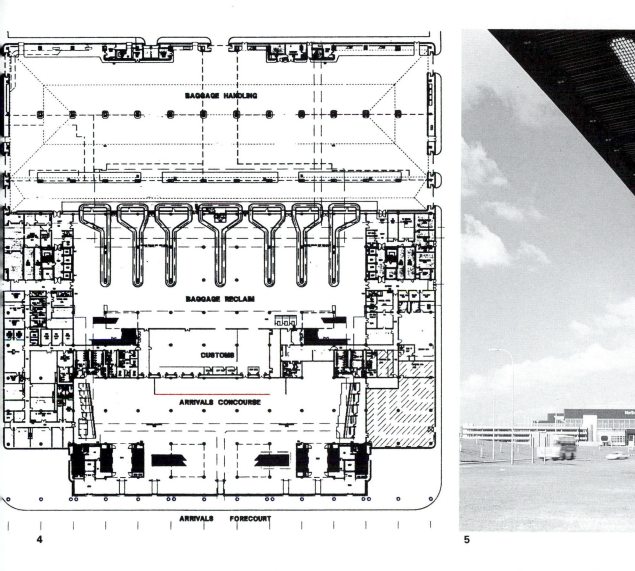

**4**    **5**

Architects YRM developed a master plan for Gatwick Airport in 1955 and since then have designed each phase of its development. The new North Terminal complex which opened in 1989 raises the airport's annual passenger-handling capacity to 25 million.

The North Terminal is essentially a very sophisticated building, designed to incorporate readily unforeseen future needs and demands. A rapid transit railway system connects it to the other airport buildings.

**1** Aerial view
**2** Typical elevation
**3** Section
**4** Plan at arrivals concourse level
**5** Railway connecting terminal buildings

# OFFICE BUILDING • HAMMERSMITH • WEST LONDON
## RALPH ERSKINE WITH LENNART BERGSTROM AND ROCK TOWNSEND

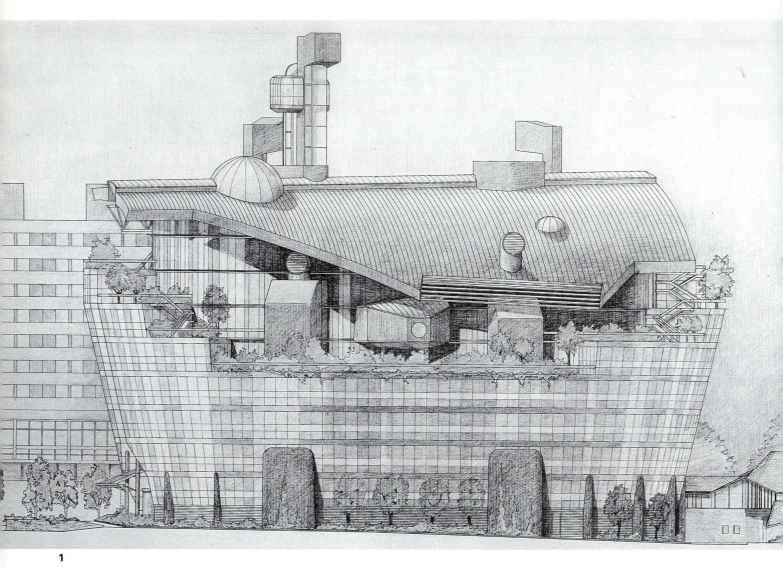

1

Ralph Erskine's office building, on an awkward very noisy site in Hammersmith, is the European headquarters for two Swedish firms. He has created a well-landscaped inward-looking environment, with office space overlooking a full-height atrium and a copper-covered roof stepping down from a nine-storey to a six-storey height.

The building has a convincing well-modelled sculptural form. Leisure and relaxation facilities for staff are located at roof level in a series of stepped landscaped terraces. The small building in the corner of the site is an urban and business studies centre for the Borough.

Built in 1990–92.

2

1 Elevation
2 General view
3 Section
4 Site plan (model)
5 Ground-floor plan

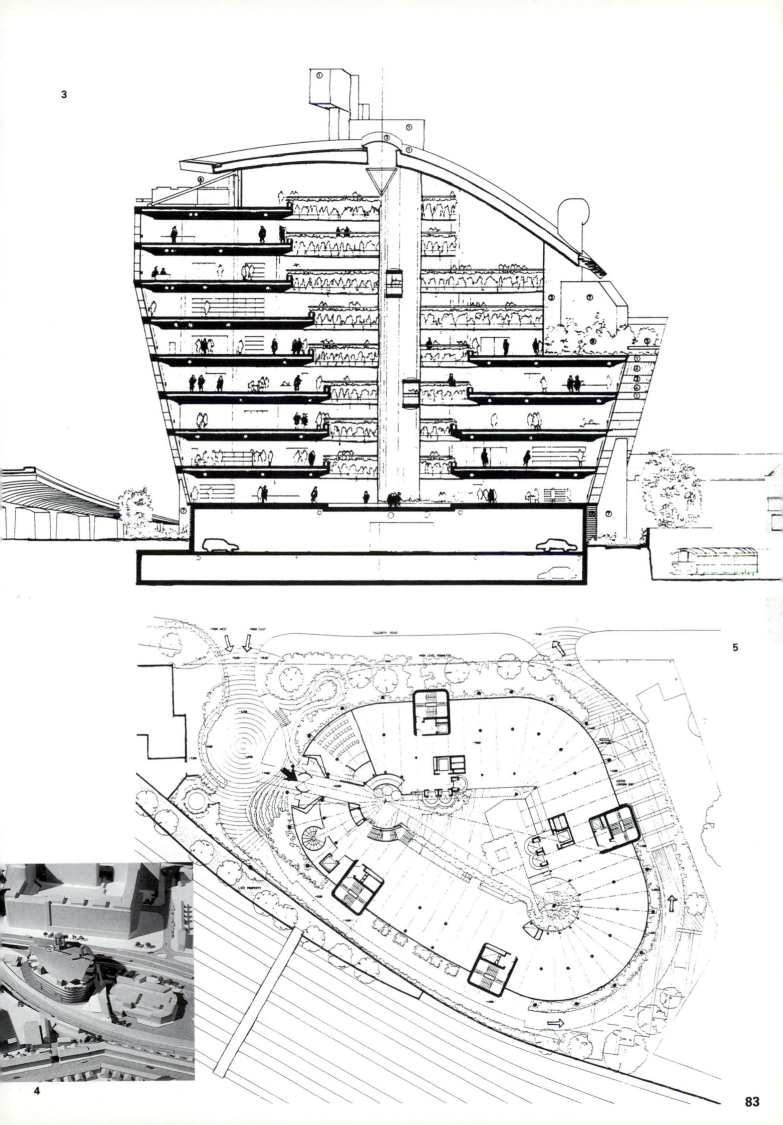

3

4

5

# MILLENNIUM TOWER • TOKYO • JAPAN
## SIR NORMAN FOSTER AND PARTNERS

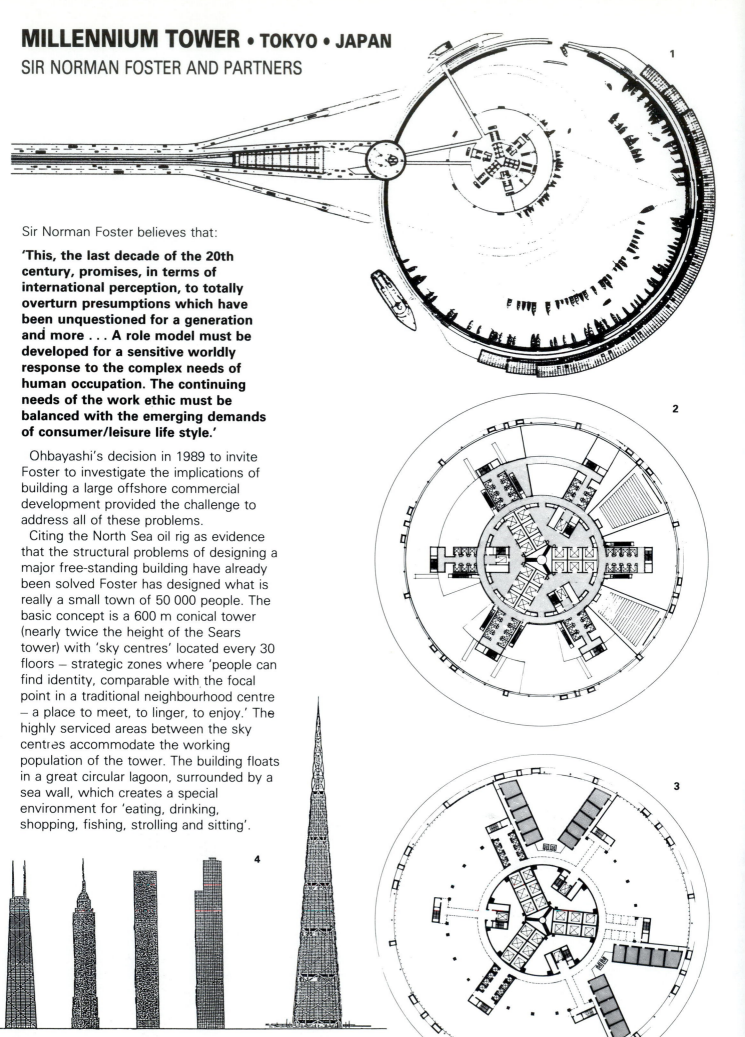

Sir Norman Foster believes that:

**'This, the last decade of the 20th century, promises, in terms of international perception, to totally overturn presumptions which have been unquestioned for a generation and more ... A role model must be developed for a sensitive worldly response to the complex needs of human occupation. The continuing needs of the work ethic must be balanced with the emerging demands of consumer/leisure life style.'**

Ohbayashi's decision in 1989 to invite Foster to investigate the implications of building a large offshore commercial development provided the challenge to address all of these problems.

Citing the North Sea oil rig as evidence that the structural problems of designing a major free-standing building have already been solved Foster has designed what is really a small town of 50 000 people. The basic concept is a 600 m conical tower (nearly twice the height of the Sears tower) with 'sky centres' located every 30 floors – strategic zones where 'people can find identity, comparable with the focal point in a traditional neighbourhood centre – a place to meet, to linger, to enjoy.' The highly serviced areas between the sky centres accommodate the working population of the tower. The building floats in a great circular lagoon, surrounded by a sea wall, which creates a special environment for 'eating, drinking, shopping, fishing, strolling and sitting'.

Hancock Tower    Empire State    World Trade    Sears Tower    600 Tower

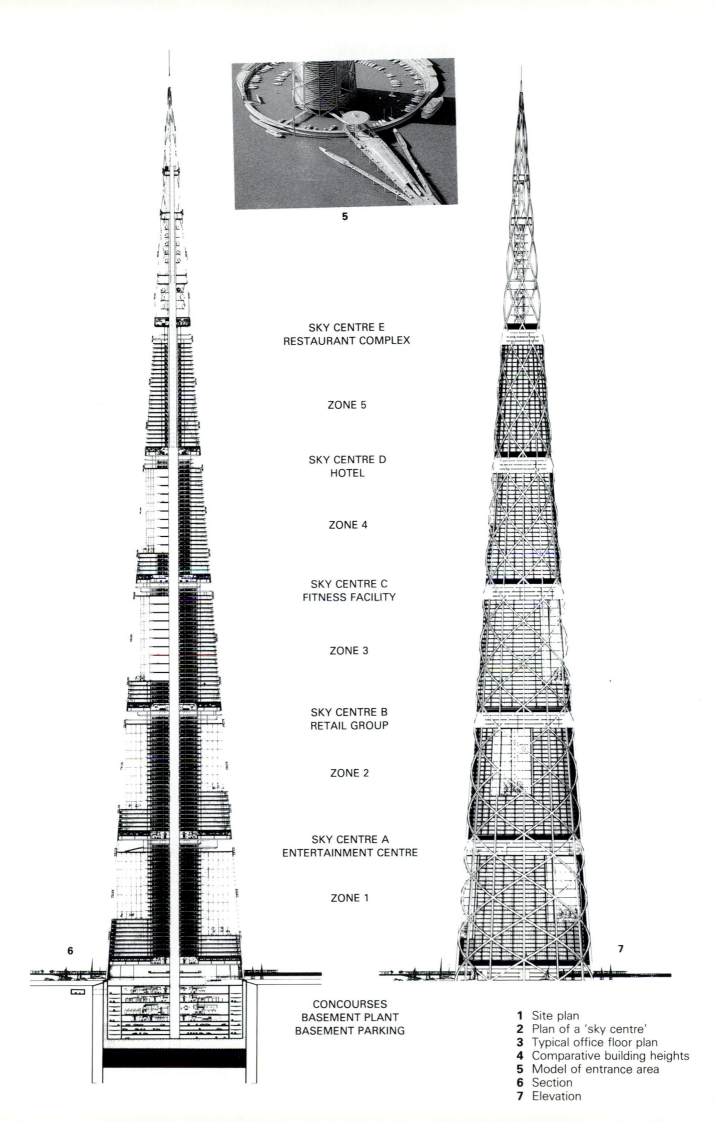

SKY CENTRE E
RESTAURANT COMPLEX

ZONE 5

SKY CENTRE D
HOTEL

ZONE 4

SKY CENTRE C
FITNESS FACILITY

ZONE 3

SKY CENTRE B
RETAIL GROUP

ZONE 2

SKY CENTRE A
ENTERTAINMENT CENTRE

ZONE 1

CONCOURSES
BASEMENT PLANT
BASEMENT PARKING

5

6

7

**1** Site plan
**2** Plan of a 'sky centre'
**3** Typical office floor plan
**4** Comparative building heights
**5** Model of entrance area
**6** Section
**7** Elevation

85

# TOKYO FORUM • COMPETITION ENTRY
## RICHARD ROGERS PARTNERSHIP

In 1985 this international competition for a major cultural centre in Tokyo
was won by the American architect Rafael Vinoly.

Many critics have admired the dramatic way in which Rogers has 'floated'
each of the three auditoria, with its attendant ancillary accommodation,
above a continuous green parkland (on the roof of a series of lower
buildings). The great sculptural forms of the auditoria are supported by tall
steel masts which dominate the overall composition as spectator
platforms.

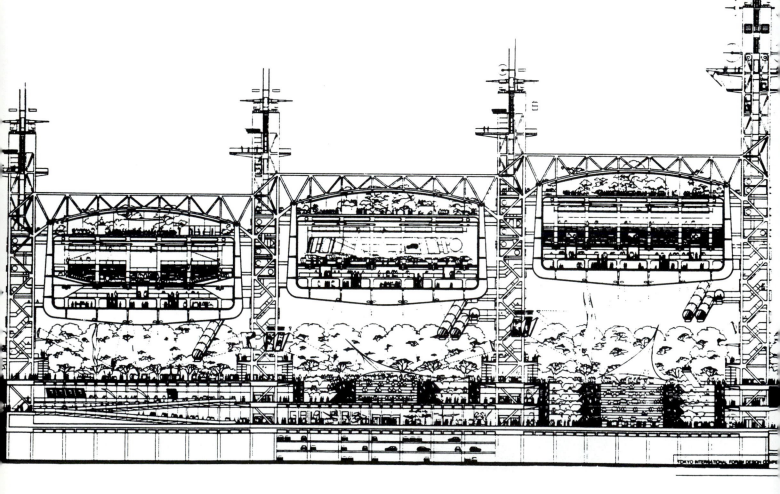

# SYDNEY FOOTBALL STADIUM • AUSTRALIA

PHILIP COX RICHARDSON TAYLOR, ARCHITECTS (Australian) •
OVE ARUP PARTNERSHIP, Engineers

1

2

Key:
1. Sports stadium
2. Tennis courts
3. Swimming pool
4. Practice field
5. Practice cricket nets
6. On-ground car park
7. Entry
8. Exit
9. S.C.G. entry/exit

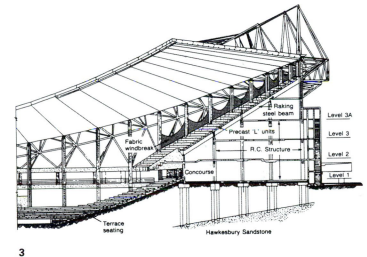

3

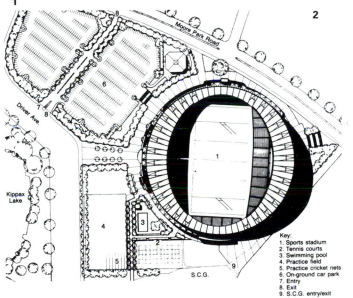

4

1 General view
2 Site plan
3 Part section
4 Part elevation

Close collaboration between architect and engineer has here resulted in a huge building of striking beauty and elegance. Here is reinforced concrete, steel and lightweight fabric used with imagination and skill to create a very worthy successor to Arups' other great achievement in Sydney, the Opera House – designed in collaboration with the Danish architect Jorn Utzon.

The stadium was opened in 1988.

# TELECOMMUNICATIONS TOWER • BARCELONA • SPAIN
## SIR NORMAN FOSTER AND PARTNERS

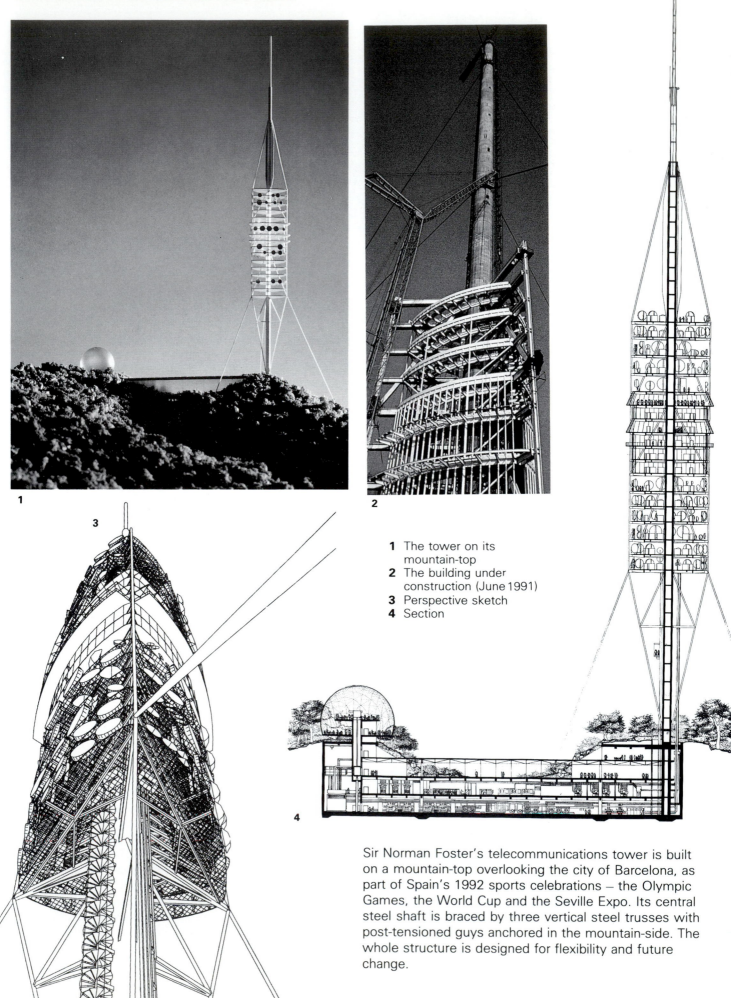

**1** The tower on its mountain-top
**2** The building under construction (June 1991)
**3** Perspective sketch
**4** Section

Sir Norman Foster's telecommunications tower is built on a mountain-top overlooking the city of Barcelona, as part of Spain's 1992 sports celebrations – the Olympic Games, the World Cup and the Seville Expo. Its central steel shaft is braced by three vertical steel trusses with post-tensioned guys anchored in the mountain-side. The whole structure is designed for flexibility and future change.

# PARIS LIBRARY • COMPETITION ENTRY
## JAN KAPLICKY and AMANDA LEVETE OF FUTURE SYSTEMS

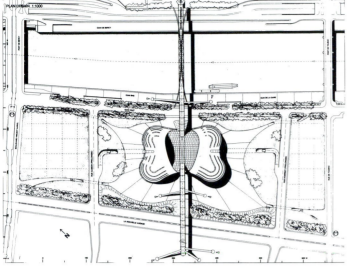

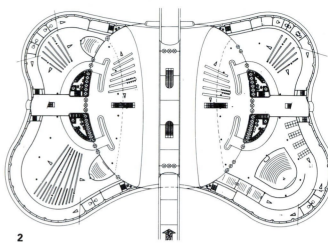

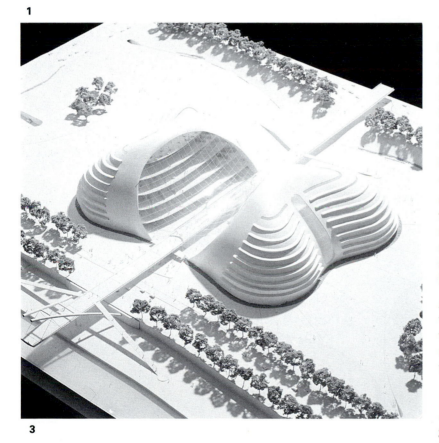

This design for Paris' 'Bibliothèque de France' won second prize in the 1989 international competition. The architects based their bold imaginative design on two hypotheses: that the familiar and accessible form of the book should be expressed, and that the growth of electronic information technology should be recognized. The design proposes

**'a smooth enveloping shell – perpetually open on the covers of a book hinged upon two vast pages of glass – to cast modulated daylight upon the new reading rooms while protecting the stores of printed and electronic knowledge beyond.'**

A new footbridge across the River Seine would pass through the library building which would be the central feature of a very large urban park stretching from the Pont de Bercy to the Pont de Tolbiac.

**1** Site plan
**2** Plan at reading room level
**3** Aerial view, looking north
**4** Section

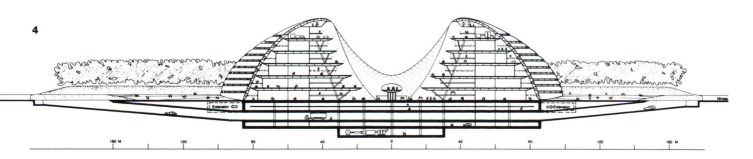

# ADVANCED TECHNOLOGY STUDIES

BRYAN AVERY

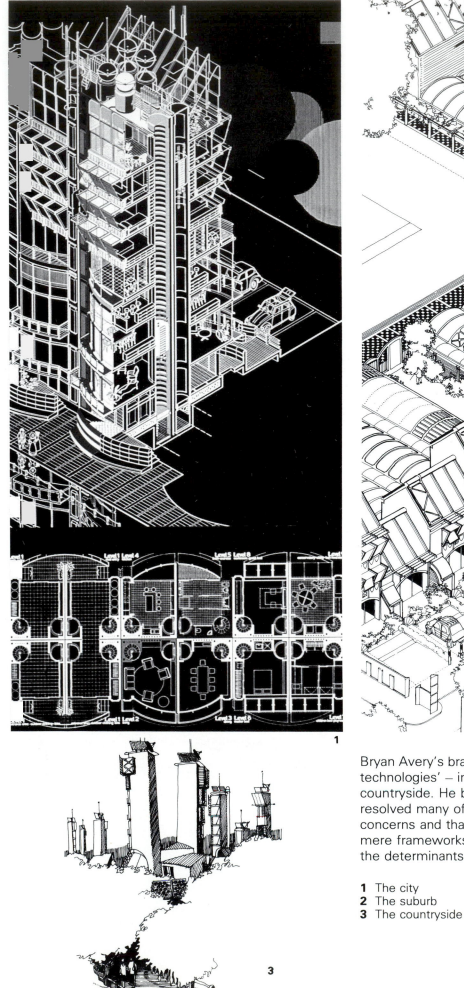

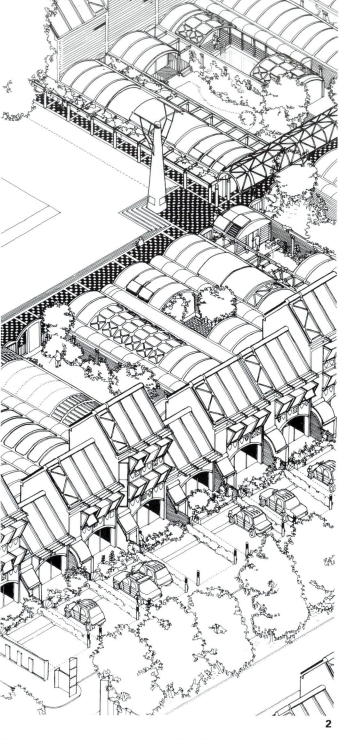

Bryan Avery's brave vision of life 'in the age of advanced technologies' — in the city, the suburb and the countryside. He believes that technology will soon have resolved many of our present social and economic concerns and that these will be seen increasingly as mere frameworks within which life takes place and not the determinants of their meanings.

1  The city
2  The suburb
3  The countryside

# 6
# CONTEXTUAL

Some British architects have been accused of designing 'sore thumbs' – buildings which are ill at ease with their neighbours, foreigners in a well-loved native environment. And this is true at the end of the century as well as at the beginning. But, happily, it is not always the case. There are a few new housing schemes in Norwich, York and one or two London boroughs where the new blends with the old in scale, character and use of materials. We have the skill and sensitivity of the city or borough architect to thank for that and sometimes the skill and sensitivity of a private architect commissioned by him.

One thinks too of the work of Arups, Powell and Moya and Richard MacCormac at Oxford and Cambridge, of the Property Services Agency architects at Kew and of Casson Conder at Basingstoke. Here harmony and contextual success have been achieved by using old traditional materials but using them in a new way to satisfy changed needs and a different way of life. Some architects – notably Sir James Stirling in the Clore Gallery, Michael Hopkins at Lord's cricket ground and Powell and Moya in the Queen Elizabeth Conference Hall opposite Westminster Abbey – have achieved this harmony and contextual success by using different materials but using them in such a way that they enhance and draw attention to the architectural qualities of their neighbours; they have in fact created harmony by contrast and the exercise of good manners.

Princess of Wales conservatory at Kew Gardens, Surrey

# STUDENTS' STUDY BEDROOMS • WORCESTER COLLEGE • OXFORD

## MacCORMAC JAMIESON PRICHARD

1 General view
2 Site plan
3 A typical interior
4 First-floor plan

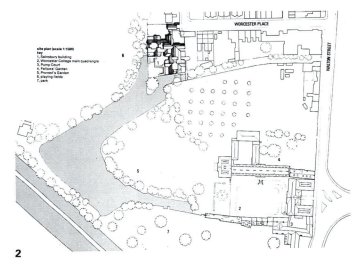

**2**

**3**

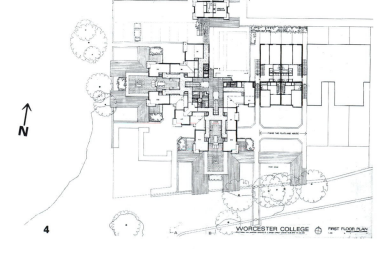

**4**

The Civic Trust award for MacCormac Jamieson Prichard's building in Oxford described it like this:

**'This light and joyful building . . . forms a romantic focus at the end of the lake and actively integrates water and building through the disposition of terraces, ramps and routes. It reinterprets the traditional Oxbridge "staircase" and invents marvellously detailed sets of study bedrooms.'**

Built in 1986.

# EARTH-SHELTERED HOUSE • TETBURY • GLOUCESTERSHIRE

## ARTHUR QUARMBY PARTNERSHIP

1

The form of this earth-sheltered house is that of an egg, with a massive stone arcade surrounding the central atrium space with its dome carried on Tuscan columns.

All the rooms in the house overlook this space. The observatory also looks outwards to a distant castle set among trees and, in the other direction, a sunken path leads to a little temple.

Levels are carefully used to create a sense of space and of repose.

Built in 1985.

1 General view
2 Section
3 Atrium
4 Floor plan

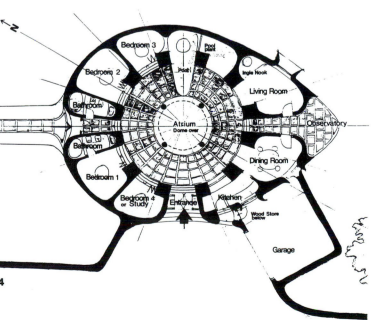

2

3

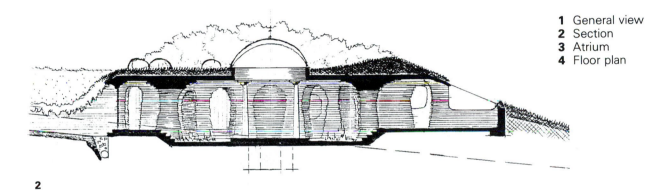

4

# MOUND STAND • LORD'S CRICKET GROUND • LONDON
## MICHAEL HOPKINS & PARTNERS

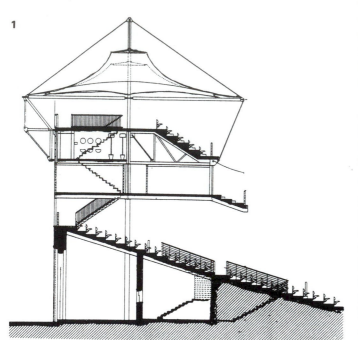

Michael Hopkins here bows to tradition. The materials are modern and the structure is innovative but the base is a restored 19th-century brick arcade (designed in 1880 by Frank Verity) and the tent roof is a modern re-interpretation of the village-green marquee.

Writing in the *Architects' Journal* in 1987 John Winter described this building – already popular with both players and spectators (even the Prince of Wales likes it) – as follows:

**'It is a layered building, and as the layers rise we are taken through the history of building technology – first, load-bearing brick with openings spanned by arches, then steel framing with concrete block infill, then a floor built as a steel box, then the polyester membranes and finally the masts and cables with flags fluttering bravely in the wind.'**

The stand was opened in 1987.

**1** Section
**2** General view
**3** Upper-level seating and roof
**4** Detail of roof structure
**5** Rear elevation
**6** Upper-level plan

**3**

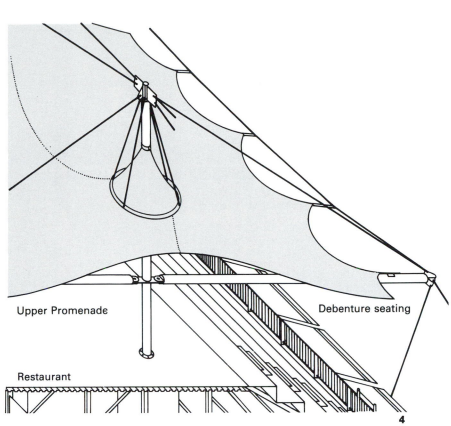

Upper Promenade

Debenture seating

Restaurant

**4**

**5**

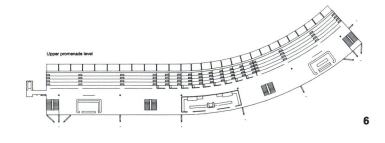

Upper promenade level

**6**

# QUEEN ELIZABETH II CONFERENCE CENTRE • WESTMINSTER • LONDON
## POWELL MOYA & PARTNERS

1

2

3

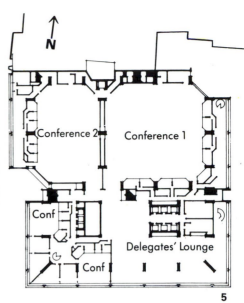

London's new conference centre forms — with its illustrious neighbours Westminster Abbey, Sanctuary Buildings, Methodist Central Hall and Middlesex Guildhall — a new Broad Sanctuary Square.

The conference floor, containing four of the conference rooms (with nine-language interpretation) and a delegate foyer, oversails the bottom three floors and is hung from cantilever beams which form a main roof line corresponding roughly with the dormers of Middlesex Guildhall and the great base of Central Hall. The top floors, housing delegates' offices, secretariat and the fifth conference room, recede northwards from the face of the conference floor. The first and second floors form a press centre. Security was a very important design consideration.

For me the siting of this building, which relates brilliantly to its neighbours, is reminiscent of the Piazza San Marco in Venice.

It was opened by the Queen in 1986.

**1** General view
**2** The new building and Big Ben
**3** Aerial perspective showing the building in its context
**4** One of the five conference rooms
**5** Third-floor plan
**6** Section

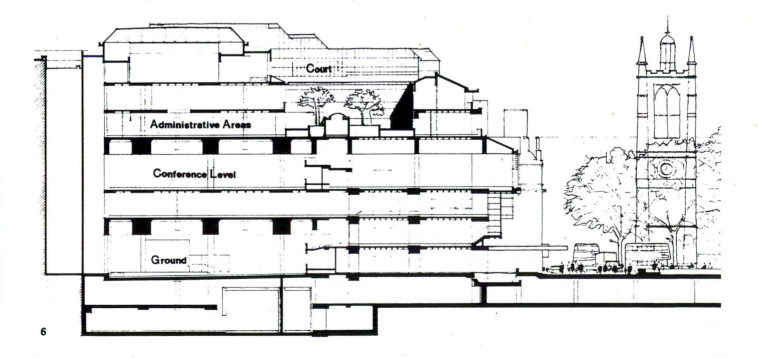

# SHADWELL BASIN HOUSING • LONDON DOCKLANDS
## MacCORMAC JAMIESON PRICHARD

1

2

3

1 Aerial view
2 Basic architectural concept
3 Four-storey flats
4 Typical elevation
5 Plans of five-storey flats

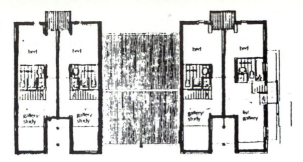

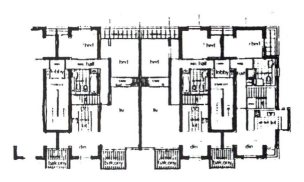

fourth floor plan

third floor plan

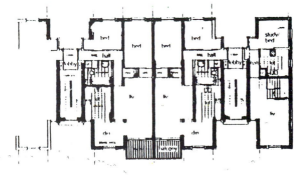

second floor plan

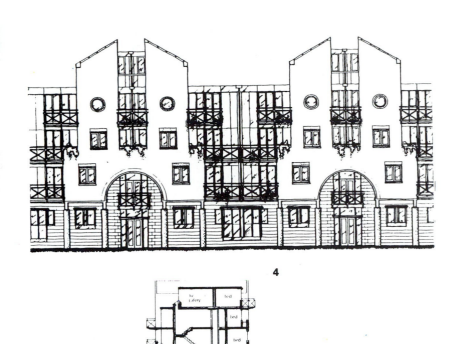

4

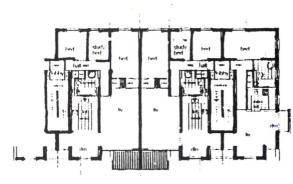

first floor plan

The architects describe their design for this — the most interesting of London Docklands' new housing — as follows:

'Shadwell Basin was the development of ideas for a domestic architecture appropriate for London's docklands, and indeed applicable to other cities' derelict docklands.

The Basin is a wonderful marine square. The urban design task was to enclose the water as effectively as possible and let the church and tree-filled churchyard play a part in the composition. The brief and the site validated the warehouse forms of large, bold buildings, deep in plan, set close to the quay edge. Warehouse-depth plans can accommodate additional flat plans with living spaces on the outside and service spaces in the dark core. Traditional Venetian palazzo plans suggested . . . the contrasting use of heavy masonry for the cellular rooms and transparent steel-framed gantry-like elevations for the living rooms.

The ground-level colonnade, with the arched entrances, inspired by the Albert Docks in Liverpool, allows a glimpse of the water from the entrance hall landing. This device gives all visitors, who must enter from the land side, a sudden and dramatic view of the Basin beyond; on entering the apartments the full prospect of the Basin is then revealed.

Our Dockland vocabulary of buildings for the scheme includes lockside houses, gate houses and dock wall houses. Much of the detailed architectural design is derived from traditional dockland artefacts, such as loading bays, crane cabins, and gantries which enlivened austere brick facades.'

Built in 1989.

ground floor plan

N

# ARTS CENTRE • WYCOMBE GIRLS' SCHOOL • BUCKINGHAMSHIRE

## GREEN LLOYD ADAMS

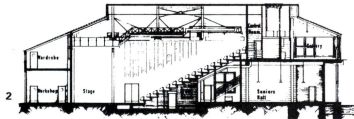

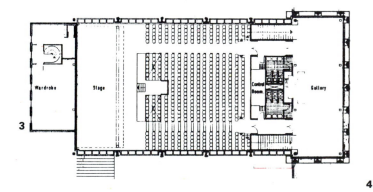

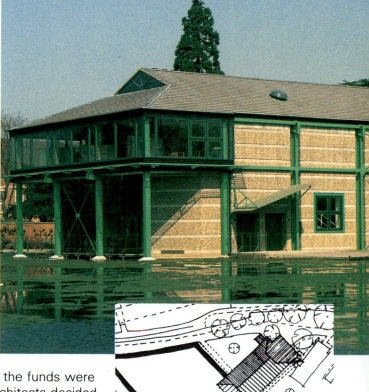

This elegant little building has been carefully located by the lakeside, with its feet in the water and a balcony inches above it. The massing and detailing of the building remind one of a traditional Japanese house. The accommodation is primarily a 500-seat theatre, with a rear-stage workshop, an upper-level gallery (with fine views over the lake) and a senior girls' hall. As the funds were very modest, the architects decided to expose the steel-and-brick structure — the steel portal frame (externally and internally) and the buff-coloured calcium silicate brickwork, with recessed courses of the same brick in grey.

Built in 1986.

1 View from lake
2 Section
3 Upper-level plan
4 Long elevation
5 Site plan

# GREENWICH MUSEUM-OF-THE-BOAT • EAST LONDON
## IAN RITCHIE ARCHITECTS

1 View from the River Thames (model)
2 Architect's concept sketch
3 Section

1

As the site for London's maritime museum was a small Thames-side park across the river from Wren's and Inigo Jones' impressive Renaissance buildings, Ian Ritchie proposed extending Wren's great axis and making it the core of his architectural composition.

This would be an exciting, active educational centre for the archaeology and reconstruction of boats. The visitor enters at the park level into the mid-space of the building and is offered the opportunity of a short- or long-route visit. The design treats handicapped people as normal visitors and everyone would enjoy the three-dimensional shapes of boats around them and witness the reconstruction and launching of boats both from within and outside the building.

The museum was designed in 1985 but, alas, was not built.

2

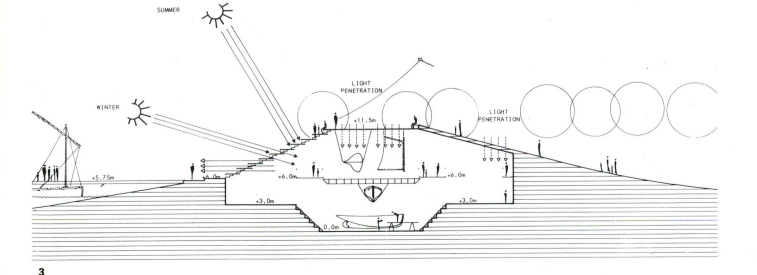

3

# PRINCESS OF WALES CONSERVATORY • KEW GARDENS • SURREY

## PROPERTY SERVICES AGENCY (GORDON WILSON)

1

This conservatory is Kew Gardens' largest and takes its place, with convincing ease and elegance, alongside well-known others designed by Burton, Nash and Chambers.

An open plan provides ten clear spaces which will be used mainly for botanical research. The basic architectural concept is a series of glazed roofs descending in receding planes to earthy terraces. In contrast to the rough Georgian-wired glass of the roofs, the vertical clear-glass walls give the impression of a huge building gradually emerging from the earth. All roofs slope at exactly the same angle, creating a sculptural rhythm which gives the building its attractive form. Glass walls and roofs are supported by an unobtrusive steel frame.

The conservatory (opened in 1989) has received several design awards.

2

1 Aerial view (opposite)
2 Roofs without walls
3 Interior
4 Roofscape
5 Glazing detail

3

4

5

# CLORE GALLERY • MILLBANK • LONDON
## SIR JAMES STIRLING, MICHAEL WILFORD & ASSOCIATES

1

The Clore Gallery is actually an extension of the Tate which is London's museum of modern art. Sir James Stirling designed it specifically to house the Tate's fine collection of paintings by J.M.W. Turner which were for many years stored in the Tate's basement. These paintings can now be seen under splendid conditions, as most of the new galleries are located on the upper floors of the new building, with natural light filtering down unobtrusively from the rooflights.

The gallery slots exceptionally well into its central London Thames-side setting and creates a new urban piazza facing the river, with a central pool which interestingly reflects the gallery's striking entrance elevation.

Stirling has in fact designed a late 20th-century building which nevertheless respects and responds to the stone neo-Renaissance Tate Gallery on one side of the site and to the red-brick former military hospital on the other. He has done this by studying the architectural detail of both buildings and echoing them in his building – in a different way.

The Clore gallery is actually phase one of a planned major extension to the Tate. It opened in 1987.

1 General view
2 Site plan
3 The two galleries
4 Plan at galleries level
5 Typical galleries
6 The new piazza
7 Sectional elevation

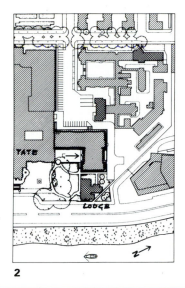

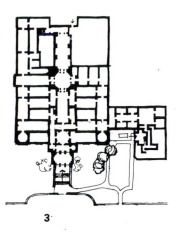

**2**

**3**

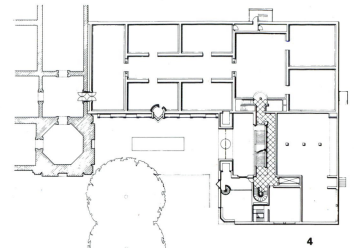

**4**

**5**

**6**

**7**

# THE BRITISH LIBRARY • ST PANCRAS • LONDON

## COLIN ST JOHN WILSON

Colin St John Wilson has designed one of Britain's major new public buildings which will house the library and reading room facilities previously scattered all over London. The building is sandwiched in between the huge bulk of St Pancras Station and a large 19th-century housing estate – to both of which it is interestingly related.

The building is divided into two sets of reading rooms (short-stay open-access and long-stay closed-access) linked by a splendid lofty entrance foyer which also gives access to an exhibition gallery and to the impressive neo-Classical King's Library transported from the British Museum. Much thought has been given to the natural lighting of the major spaces in the building and this has been outstandingly successful.

In homage to Gilbert Scott's formidable St Pancras Hotel, red-brick wall facings and dark grey slate roof coverings were specified.

In this library the architect has created three – or perhaps four – impressive interior spaces with a powerful sculptural ambience; Berlage would have loved them. Wilson has also given Londoners a welcome new urban square opening on to the Euston Road.

Phase one is expected to open in 1994.

1

2

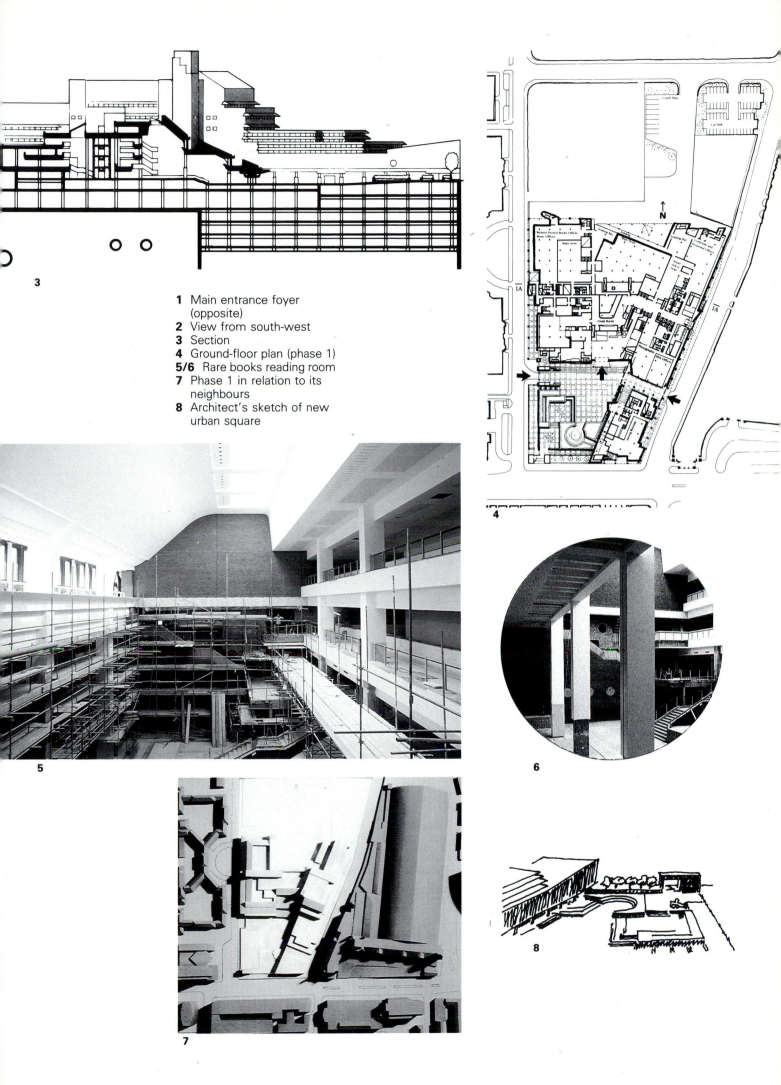

1 Main entrance foyer (opposite)
2 View from south-west
3 Section
4 Ground-floor plan (phase 1)
5/6 Rare books reading room
7 Phase 1 in relation to its neighbours
8 Architect's sketch of new urban square

# OFFICE BUILDING • VICTORIA • LONDON
## RICHARD HORDEN

1

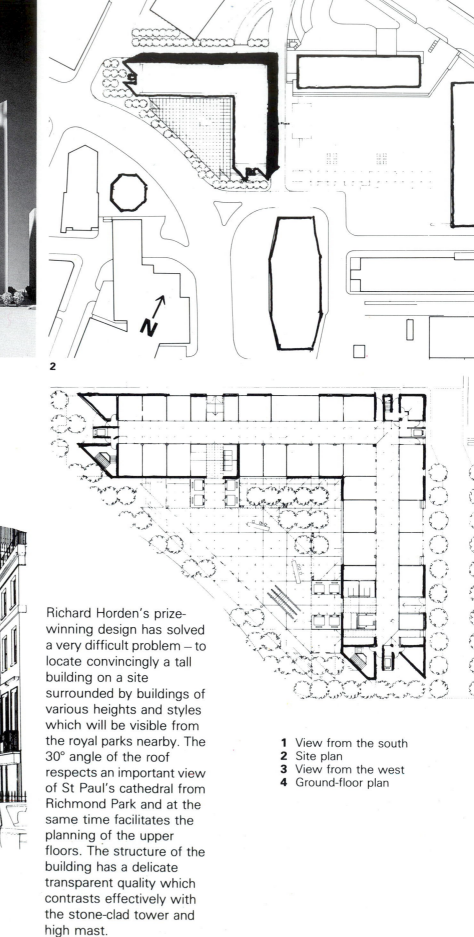

2

Richard Horden's prize-winning design has solved a very difficult problem – to locate convincingly a tall building on a site surrounded by buildings of various heights and styles which will be visible from the royal parks nearby. The 30° angle of the roof respects an important view of St Paul's cathedral from Richmond Park and at the same time facilitates the planning of the upper floors. The structure of the building has a delicate transparent quality which contrasts effectively with the stone-clad tower and high mast.

Built 1990–94.

4

**1** View from the south
**2** Site plan
**3** View from the west
**4** Ground-floor plan

3

# BASINGSTOKE CIVIC OFFICES • HAMPSHIRE
## CASSON CONDER PARTNERSHIP

1

Built in 1992, this building is convincingly well related to its neighbours, to existing site features and to the park. The pedestrian approach to the civic group has determined the very human scale of the new building.

1 General view
2 Section
3 Ground-floor plan
4 Site plan
5 Courtyard

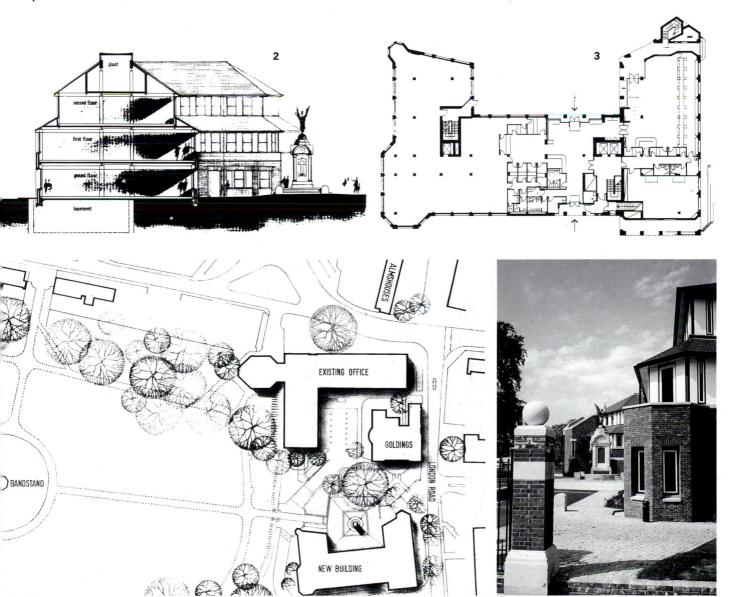

4

5

# A NEW GORBALS NEIGHBOURHOOD · GLASGOW
## CAMPBELL ZOGOLOVITCH WILKINSON GOUGH

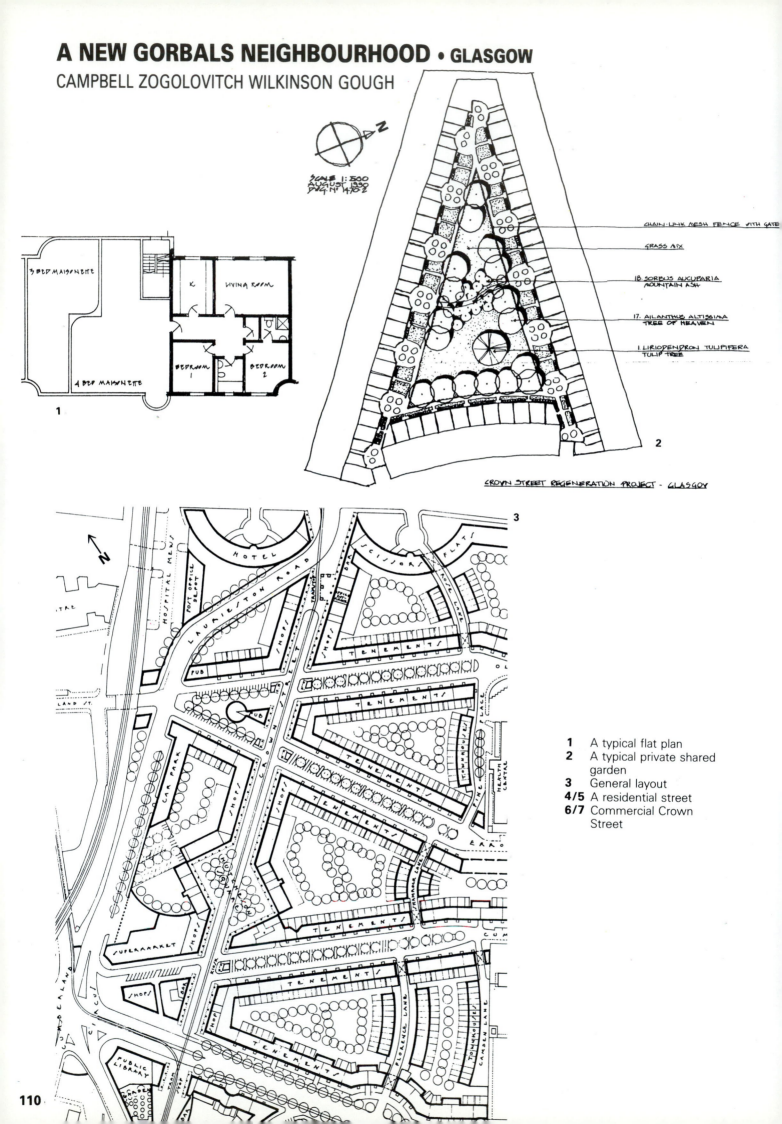

CROWN STREET REGENERATION PROJECT - GLASGOW

1 A typical flat plan
2 A typical private shared garden
3 General layout
4/5 A residential street
6/7 Commercial Crown Street

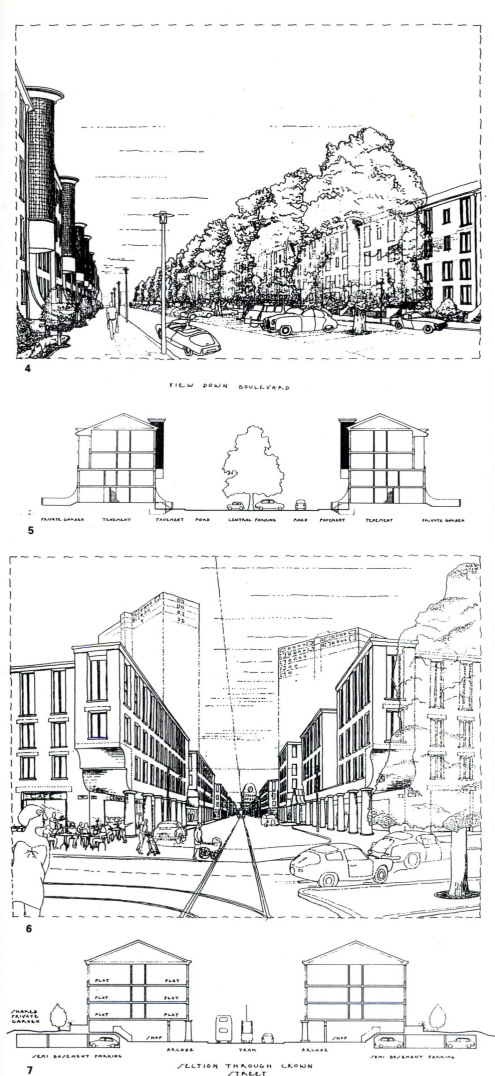

**4**

VIEW DOWN BOULEVARD

**5**

PRIVATE GARDEN   TENEMENT   PAVEMENT   ROAD   CENTRAL PARKING   ROAD   PAVEMENT   TENEMENT   PRIVATE GARDEN

**6**

CAFE

**7**

SHARED PRIVATE GARDEN   FLAT FLAT FLAT FLAT FLAT FLAT   SHOP   ARCADE   TRAM   ARCADE   SHOP

SEMI BASEMENT PARKING   SECTION THROUGH CROWN STREET   SEMI BASEMENT PARKING

These proposals for the regeneration of a run-down area of Glasgow won the 1990 competition organized by the City Corporation.

The proposals are based on the acceptance of two major facts: the street, which is 'the ubiquitous urban space of Glasgow'; and the tenement block, which has proved itself to be 'the resilient Glaswegian form of housing, but which can however be adapted to be more suitable for family life at ground level and with private outside spaces' – reminiscent of London's Maida Vale gardens.

The architects' proposed street is a wide boulevard, with trees in the centre and car parking beneath them. Their private outside space is a shared well-landscaped garden formed by the tenement blocks themselves. The commercial Crown Street is more formal, with the tramway in the centre and shops set back behind a pedestrian arcade.

The whole informal layout of streets and urban blocks is skilfully woven into the street pattern of the surrounding area, so that it is in fact a logical 21st-century extension of Glasgow's traditional urban form.

Work on site started in 1992. The anticipated completion date is 1997.

# ZWOLSESTRAAT MULTI-USE PROJECT • SCHEVENINGEN • HOLLAND
## NEAVE BROWN & DAVID PORTER

The site for this large development is bisected by a straight very busy street which leads, via the sea-front, to The Hague. It is on the northern edge of the town, facing the dunes and very near the sea-front.

High-density social and luxury housing is proposed (500 dwellings), car parking for residents, separate parking for tourists (2000 cars), a petrol station, a students hostel for the hotel school and commercial accommodation at the west end. A major feature of the design is the separation of the circulation of residents and tourists – a client requirement – resulting in a glazed arcade running the whole length of the site.

Two main factors have determined the form of the buildings: the city role of Zwolsestraat serving the vast numbers of tourists; and the abrupt contrasts between the new large scale of 'Anywhere town' and the local quiet residential scale; and also the romantic quality of the dunes.

A close look at these proposals shows that they respect the existing grain of the city and respond to the character of each area, to Zwolsestraat itself and to the wild dunes.

Construction of the first building (the students hostel) began in 1990.

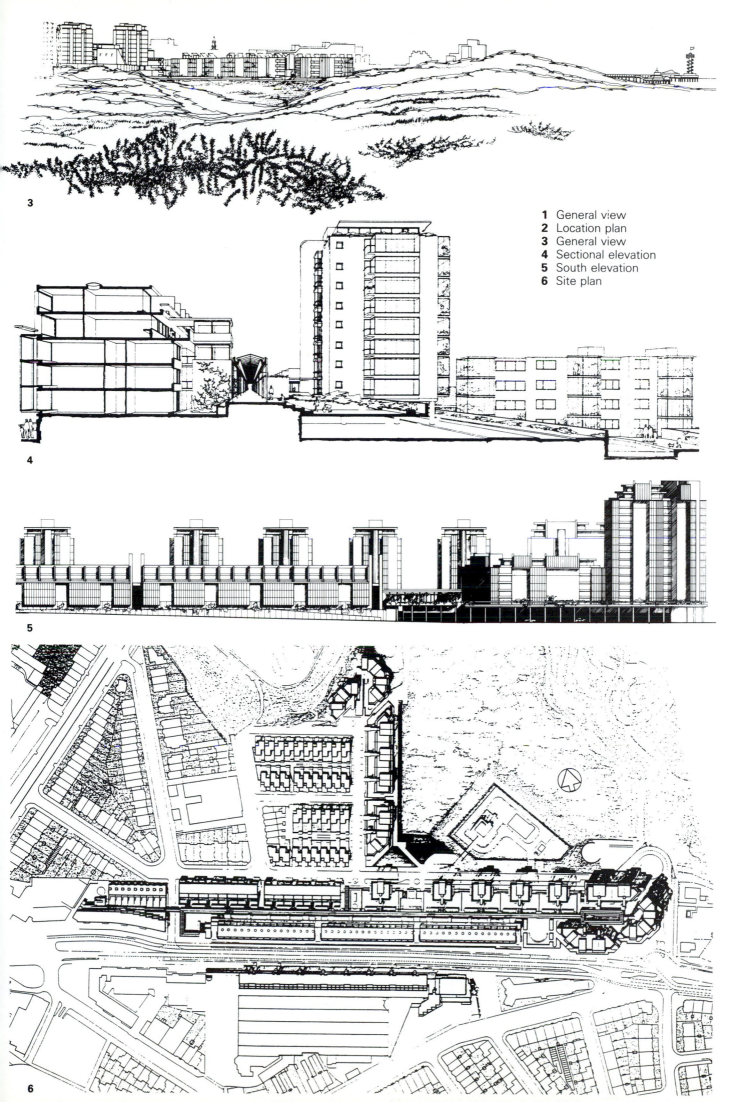

**3**

1 General view
2 Location plan
3 General view
4 Sectional elevation
5 South elevation
6 Site plan

**4**

**5**

**6**

# KING'S CROSS PARK · LONDON
## SIR NORMAN FOSTER AND PARTNERS

**1**

**2**

**Masterplan
October
1989**

**3**

New British Rail station
on the North London
Line

Light industrial
buildings

Housing

Offices

Shops

Open parkland

Housing

Victorian buildings for
leisure/community
facilities

Housing

Regent's Canal

Natural park

St Pancras Gas Holders

East Park Way

West Park Drive

King's Cross station

New concourse
building linking the
two stations

St Pancras station

New civic space

**4**

**5**

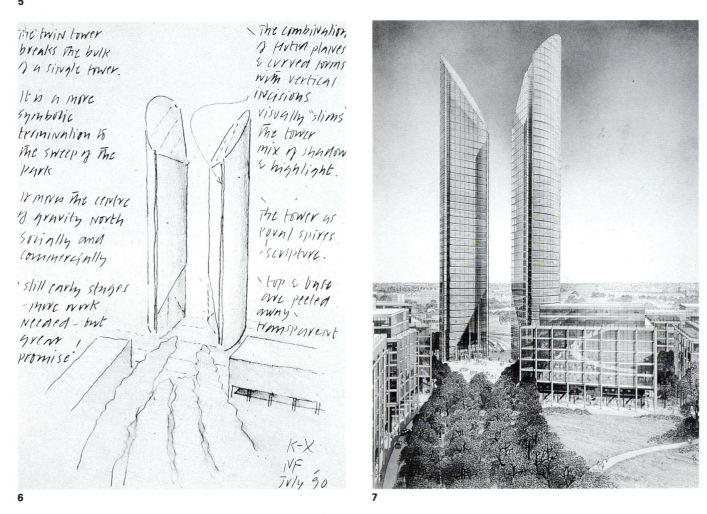

**6**

**7**

The twin tower breaks the bulk of a single tower.

It is a more symbolic termination to the sweep of the park

It moves the centre of gravity north socially and commercially

still early stages - more work needed - but great promise!

The combination of flatter planes & curved forms with vertical incisions visually "slims" the tower mix of shadow & highlight.

The tower as royal spires - sculpture.

top & base are peeled away - transparent

K-X
NF
July 90

The importance of green space to a city is reflected in London's long tradition of parks and gardens. Sir Norman Foster's first master plan (in 1987) for the redevelopment of this huge 120-acre (48.5 ha) site (the former goods yard area north of King's Cross and St Pancras stations) suggested an oval park, with listed Victorian buildings and gas holders in its centre, the Regents Canal flowing through it, and a mixture of offices, residential and shopping around its perimeter; it also located the new London terminal for the Channel Tunnel trains between the two stations, with a gigantic glass vault over it.

Since 1987 the master plan has undergone many changes, the most significant being the replacement of a cluster of office towers by an elegant pair of very tall glass towers in the northern area of the site, carefully located to protect views of St Paul's cathedral from the north, and a redesign of the Channel Tunnel terminal on its very awkward site.

# GULBENKIAN GALLERY OF MODERN ART • LISBON • PORTUGAL
## SIR LESLIE MARTIN WITH PROFESSOR IVOR RICHARDS

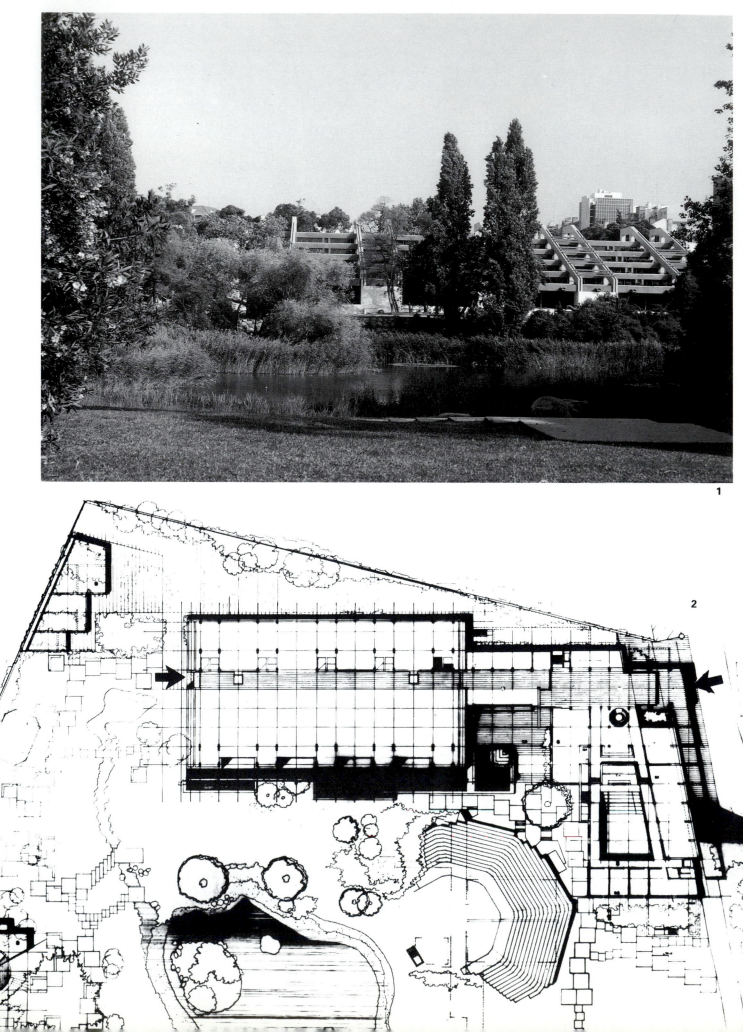

1

2

3

The Gulbenkian Gallery in Lisbon takes its place within the setting of a splendid park. Its stepped roof provides the appropriate interior volumes for different types of exhibit and reduces the scale in the garden frontage. The planted roof levels extend the garden actually over the building itself. It is a building in a landscape.

The park was actually redesigned and now includes a lake (seen from inside the auditorium) and an outdoor amphitheatre which is used during the summer months.

The stepped roof, with its huge exposed trusses, gives the main building a powerful dramatic form, but – in spite of this – it fits gracefully and naturally into its parkland setting.

The gallery was opened in 1983, and in 1992 was recipient of the RIBA trustees medal.

4

1 The main building in its park setting
2 Principal floor plan, with the animation building bottom right
3 Elevation to the park
4 Section, showing the stepped roof, with external trusses, north lighting and roof planting

# 'A GATEWAY TO VENICE' COMPETITION 1991
## JEREMY DIXON • EDWARD JONES • BDP ARCHITECTS

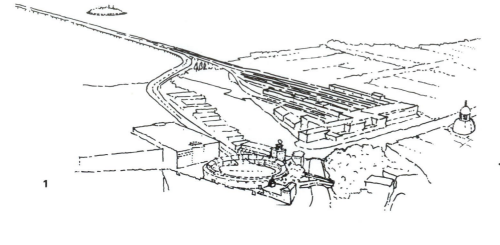

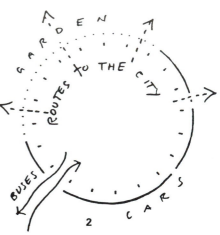

The architects won an international competition in 1991 for 'A gateway for Venice' building which would solve the urgent and difficult problem of the arrival in island Venice of large numbers of buses, via the causeway from the mainland.

Unlike the giant Fiat car garage nearby, this bus garage – in spite of its huge size – fits unobtrusively into its subtle Venetian environment.

The building takes the form of a continuous open concrete colonnade, supporting a glass and steel cantilevered canopy that was inspired by the traditional Italian street umbrella. The circular form arises as a mechanical solution to the problem of organizing the movement of buses, and, historically, is a reminder of the Colosseum, the Circus Maximus and the Greek amphitheatres. Internally the circular form is clear and uncompromising. Externally the circle is obscured by existing buildings and a few new ones fronting the Grand Canal on one side and the existing park on the other. Whereas buses enter through a single opening in the curved wall, pedestrians have many ways of leaving the building. All pedestrian facilities are arranged along the perimeter of the building.

Full marks to the architects for a highly imaginative design detail: rain falls from the inner edge of the canopy (no gutters or RWPs) in the form of a cylindrical wall of droplets, through which only the buses have to penetrate.

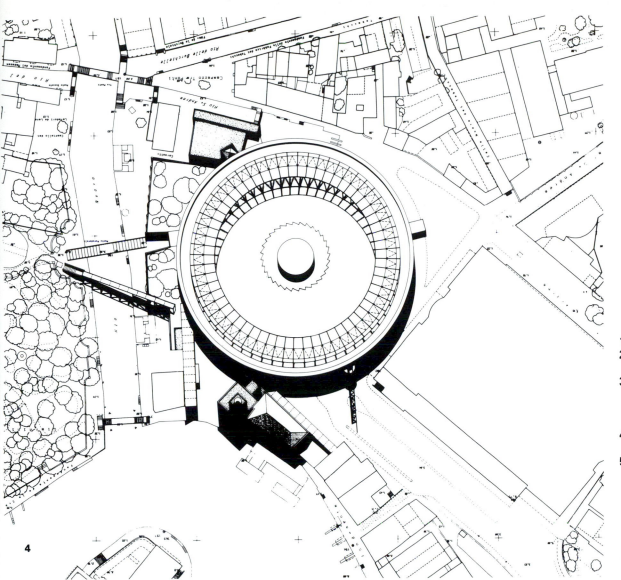

1 Location plan
2 Basic circulation plan
3 Aerial view (model), with the Grand Canal in the foreground
4 The building in its Venetian context
5 The pedestrian circulation area

4

5

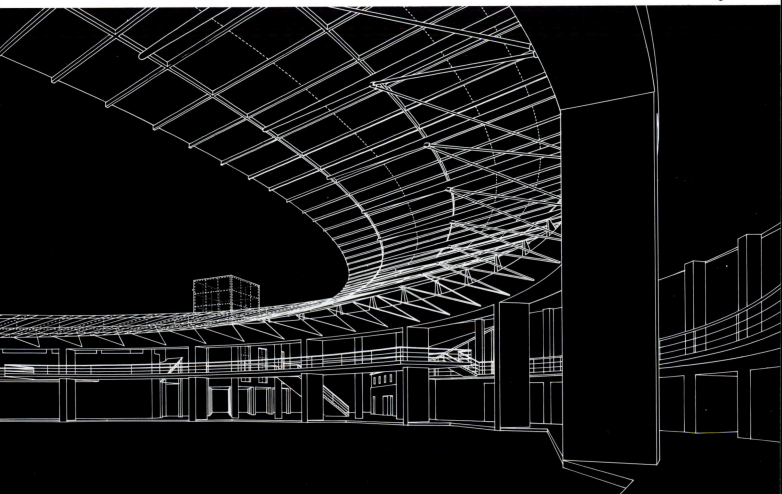

# FOUNTAINS ABBEY VISITORS' CENTRE • YORKSHIRE
## EDWARD CULLINAN ARCHITECTS

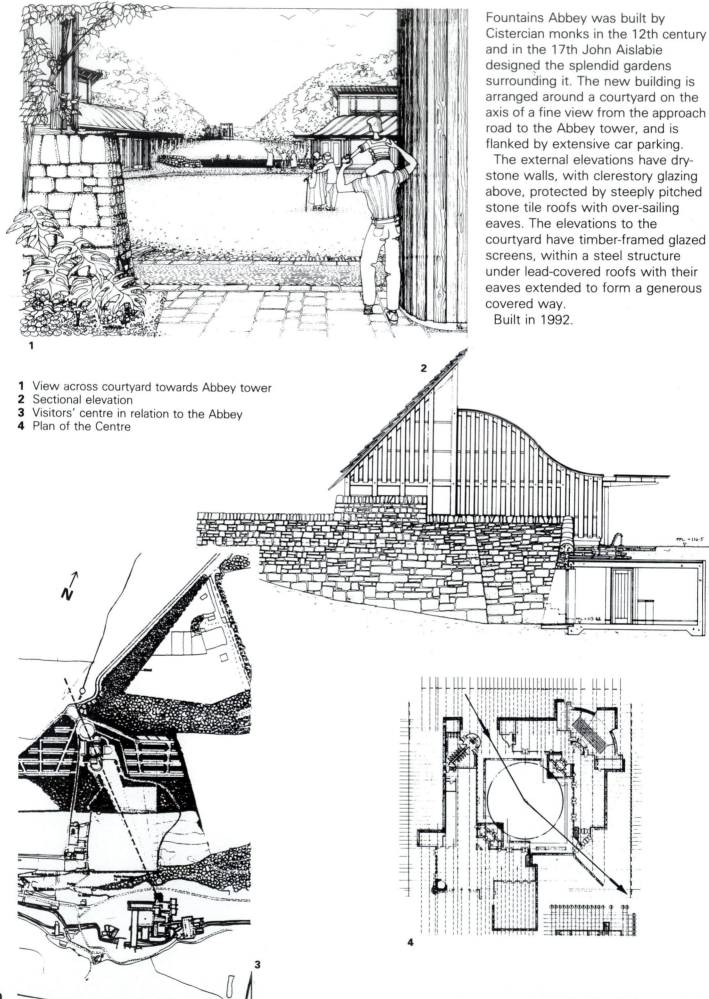

Fountains Abbey was built by Cistercian monks in the 12th century and in the 17th John Aislabie designed the splendid gardens surrounding it. The new building is arranged around a courtyard on the axis of a fine view from the approach road to the Abbey tower, and is flanked by extensive car parking.

The external elevations have dry-stone walls, with clerestory glazing above, protected by steeply pitched stone tile roofs with over-sailing eaves. The elevations to the courtyard have timber-framed glazed screens, within a steel structure under lead-covered roofs with their eaves extended to form a generous covered way.

Built in 1992.

1 View across courtyard towards Abbey tower
2 Sectional elevation
3 Visitors' centre in relation to the Abbey
4 Plan of the Centre

# 7
# FUN

Many people who dislike modern architecture will tell you that they find it dull, bleak, inhuman, uninteresting. Much of it is. They will remind you that modern art is often stimulating, provocative, exciting, fun; and they will mention the paintings of Joan Miró, Paul Klee and Stanley Spencer. So why should so much modern architecture be so very dull? What about the Brighton Pavilion and Disneyland?

Today, as the number of working hours per week steadily decreases and the number of leisure hours increases, people have to be entertained and amused in new ways. Here is the architect's opportunity to introduce fun into his or her work – as they design the new leisure and recreation centres, the big shopping malls and superstores, the family swimming pools and holiday camps which are becoming a major feature of our way of living and behaving today – and also of course in the design of restaurants, cafés, bars and infants schools.

A restaurant car park in Wisconsin

Brighton Pavilion

# WOKING POOL-IN-THE PARK • SURREY
## FAULKNER BROWNS ARCHITECTS

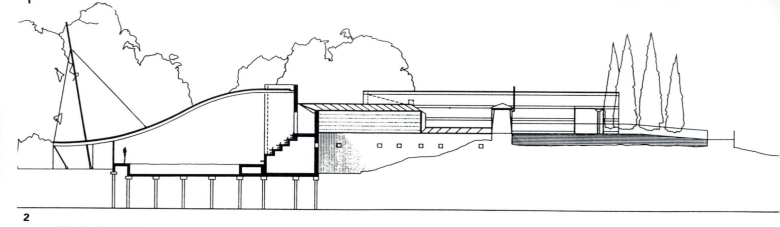

The Woking leisure centre has been extended by Faulkner Browns, with two swimming pools and well-planned spectator facilities, entered from a fine new 'rotunda' which successfully links new and existing. The dramatic playful appearance of the sweeping roof cascading down into the park forms an interesting counterpoint with a row of tall steel masts.

Built in 1988.

**1** General view from park
**2** Sectional elevation
**3** Structural detail
**4** First-floor plan
**5** Interior
**6** Site plan

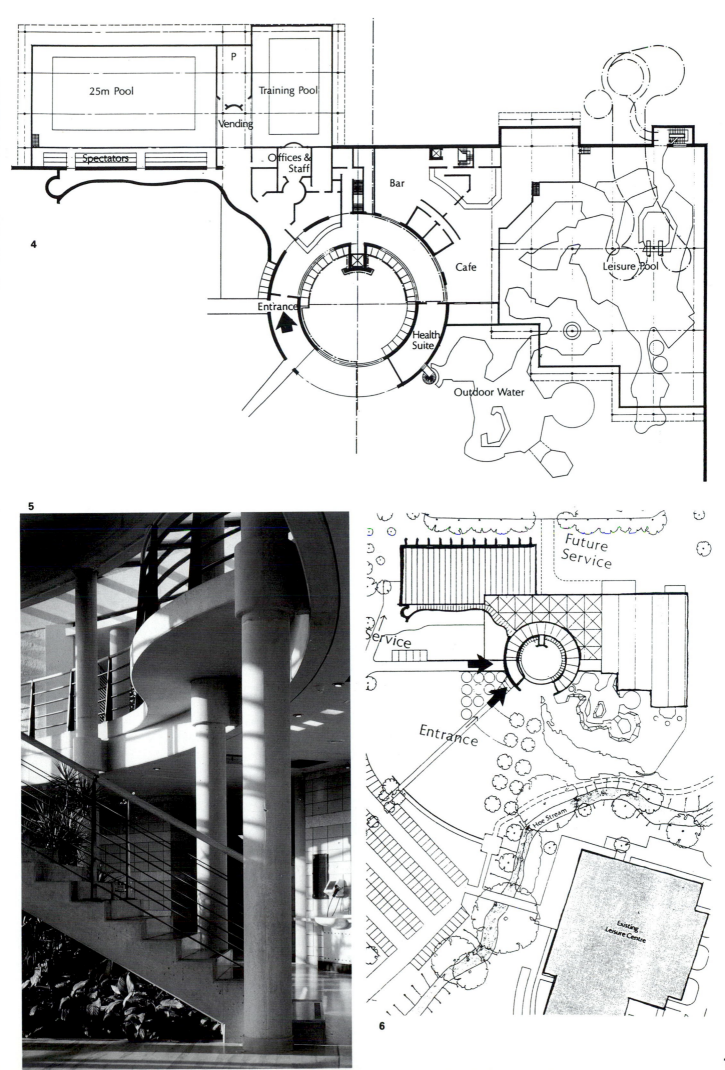

**4**

25m Pool

P

Training Pool

Vending

Spectators

Offices & Staff

Bar

Cafe

Leisure Pool

Entrance

Health Suite

Outdoor Water

**5**

**6**

Future Service

Service

Entrance

Hoe Stream

Existing Leisure Centre

# BIENNALE BOOKSHOP • VENICE • ITALY

## SIR JAMES STIRLING, MICHAEL WILFORD & ASSOCIATES, WITH TOM MUIRHEAD

**1**

**2**

**1** General view
**2** Location plan, in the Biennale park
**3** Site plan
**4** Plan of bookshop
**5** Interior
**6** Cross-section

The Venice Biennale's new bookshop replaces one destroyed by fire some years ago. It is long and narrow — sandwiched in between two parallel rows of trees leading from the waterfront to the very large Italian pavilion. It is a fun building (the architects call it 'a bookshop–boatshop') and its boat-like form has certainly been inspired by Venice's *vaporetti*.

Entrance to the building is marked by an illuminated roof-top drum from which a laser sends beams of coloured light through the overhanging tree branches into the sky — a marker visible from the lagoon. The sloping roof is sheathed in copper, its overhanging eaves projecting over the boardwalk which runs around the three glazed sides of the building, through which all the books and catalogues can be seen laid out on a continuous bench 40 m long.

The bookshop–boatshop opened its doors in September 1991.

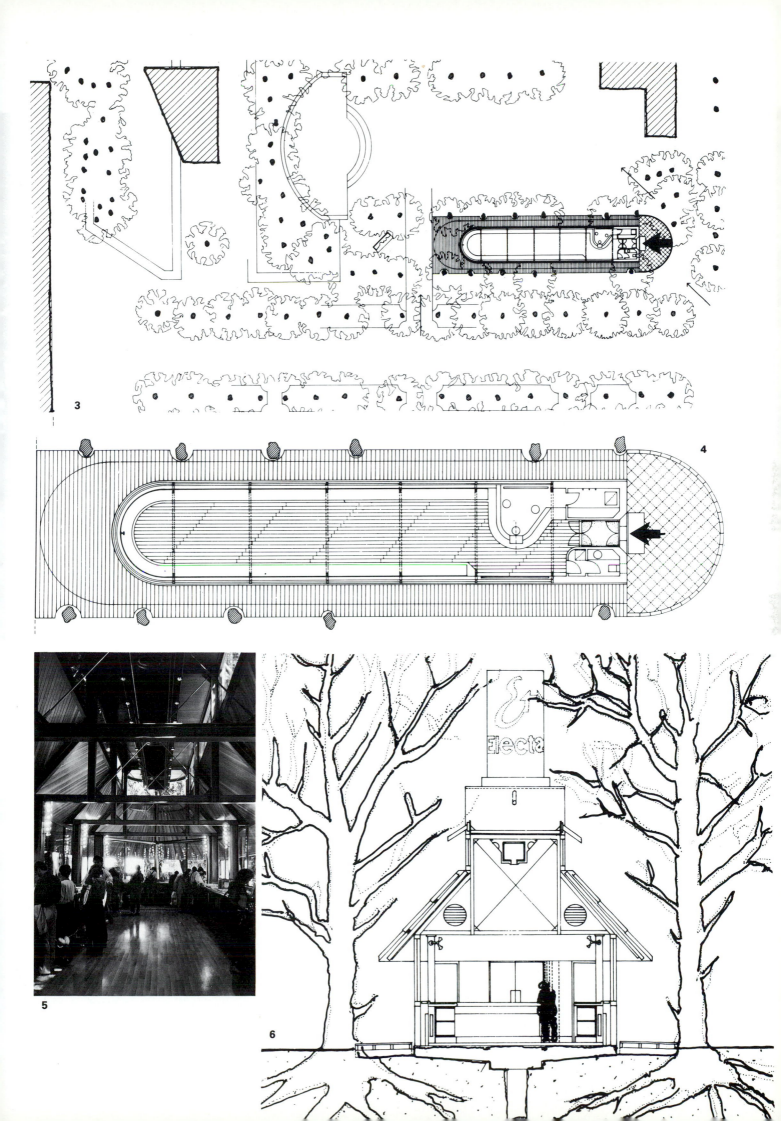

3

4

5

6

# WONDERWORLD THEME PARK • NORTHAMPTONSHIRE
## DEREK WALKER ASSOCIATES

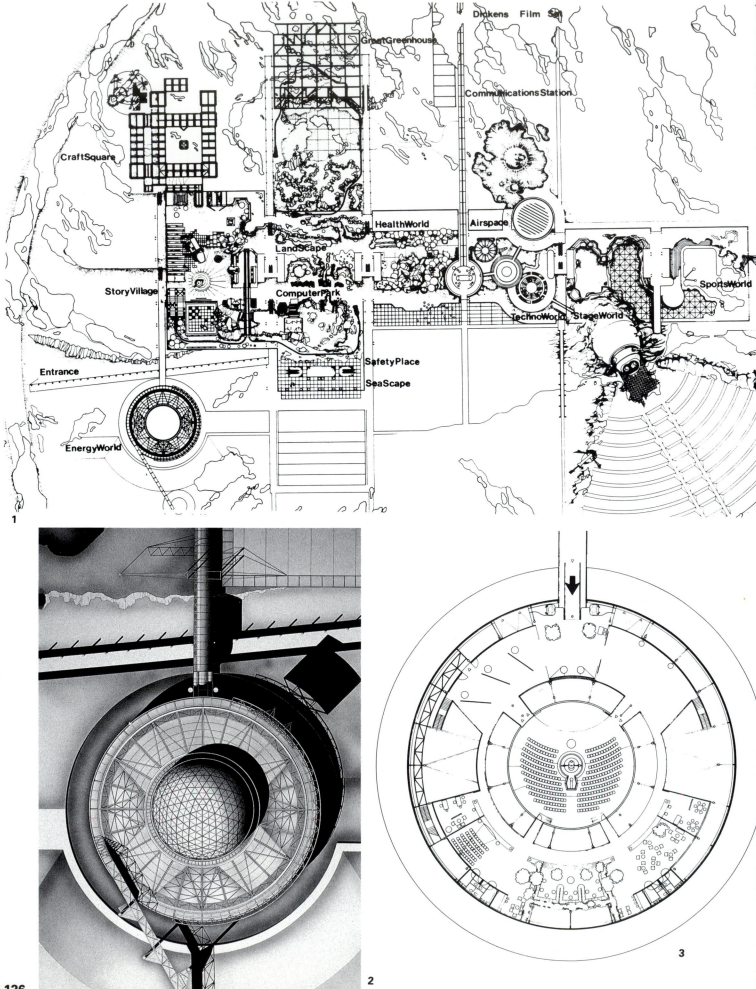

1

2

3

The WonderWorld complex is Britain's largest leisure and recreation theme park, with an expected annual attendance of 4.8 million. It will offer 13 major themed areas using the latest simulation technology in a year-round climate-controlled environment. Nine of these will be housed in a single major structure, the Central Pavilion, 450 m long with 94 000 m² of covered space on two levels under a suspended steel and glass canopy.

The Central Pavilion and its outlying pavilions – CraftSquare, LandScape, EnergyWorld and Communications Station – are grouped at the focus of the ThemeBowl, a man-made dish 700 m in diameter.

The ThemeBowl is itself the centrepiece of a complex covering 1000 acres (400 ha), incorporating a championship golf course and nature reserve, theme-related industrial development, a shopping centre, luxury housing, a sports area, an entrance plaza, a hospitality area, a system of roads and infrastructure and parking for 21 000 cars.

Work started on site in 1992. The anticipated completion date is 1995.

**4**

1 Layout of park
2/3 EnergyWorld building: model and floor plan
4 Entrance to sports hall
5 Interior of EnergyWorld
6 Structural model of Central Pavilion
7 Section through Omnimax theatre
8 Section through concert hall

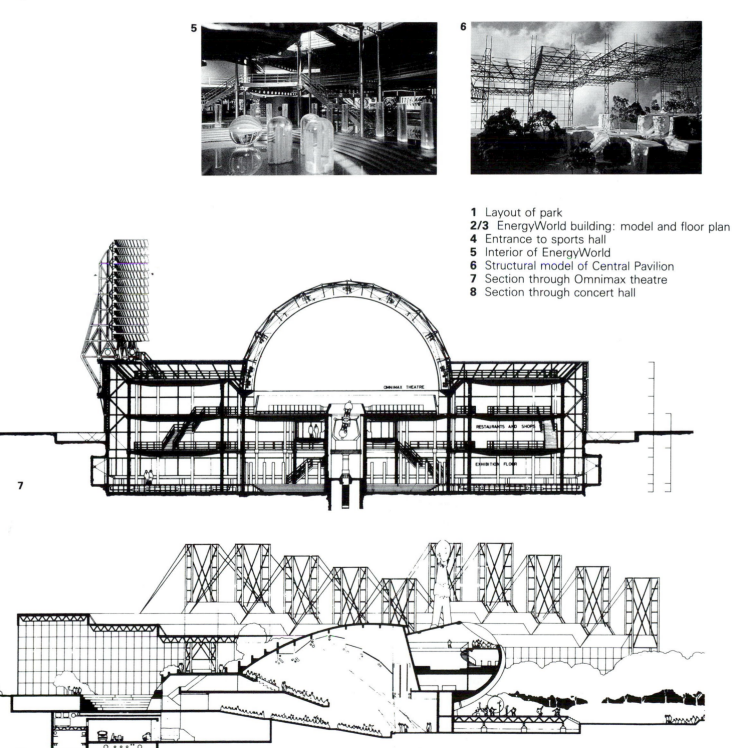

# EXETER 'SKYPARK' • DEVON

## RENTON HOWARD WOOD LEVIN

**1**

**2**

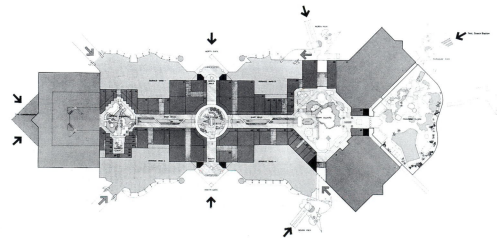

**3**

**1** Central building
**2** Elevation
**3** Plan

Exeter's leisure centre is located immediately beside the airport. Its 97-ha site is well landscaped, with a dominant 'waterpark' giving visitors all kinds of 'organic fun', and a large central building

the central building are the interweaving of the various floors and the huge roof which is a translucent fabric stretched on tension cables.

Work is expected to start on site in the mid-1990s.

full of fun-fair amusement facilities and some commercial accommodation.

The park also contains the airport's terminal building, offices, shops and a hotel.

The two main features of

# HOUSE IN CLERKENWELL • LONDON

## CAMPBELL ZOGOLOVITCH WILKINSON GOUGH

### 1st Floor

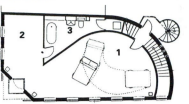

1 Master Bedroom
2 Dressing Room
3 Bathroom

### 2nd Floor

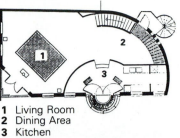

1 Living Room
2 Dining Area
3 Kitchen

### 3rd Floor

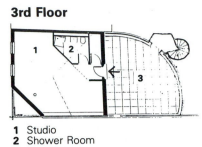

1 Studio
2 Shower Room
3 Roof Terrace

### Ground Floor

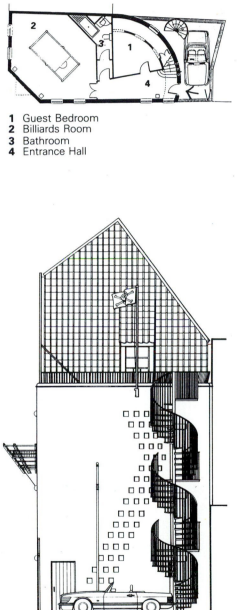

1 Guest Bedroom
2 Billiards Room
3 Bathroom
4 Entrance Hall

1 Floor plans
2 General view of the house
3 Entrance elevation

A fun house designed by CZWG for a well-known BBC TV personality.

It is built on a corner site in a district which has a mediaeval street pattern. It has four floors with a roof terrace. Access to the terrace is by a separate outside staircase which also leads to the roof-top studio with splendid views over London.

Built in 1988.

129

# ISLE OF DOGS PUMPING STATION • EAST LONDON

## JOHN OUTRAM ASSOCIATES

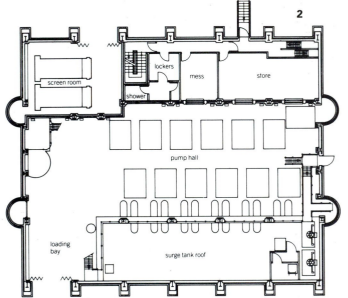

1

John Outram's approach to design is highly individualistic; he has described it as 'popular Classic'. He uses ordinary materials like brick, steel and concrete but uses them in a colourful, sculptural and unique way. His pumping station on the Isle of Dogs epitomizes his rationalistic but very expressive approach to design. The plan of the building is simply one large space, housing pumping machinery, but the elevations are colourful and strongly modelled – dominated by huge semicircular columns which are in fact services ducts.

The building – completed in 1988 – is already a notable East End landmark.

2

**1** General view
**2** Plan
**3** Entrance elevation
**4** Interior

3

4

# WAVERLEY MARKET CENTRE • EDINBURGH
## BUILDING DESIGN PARTNERSHIP

1

The Waverley Market Centre has already become a popular gathering-place for Edinburgh's shoppers. It is situated below street level so as not to disturb views of the low-lying Waverley Gardens from Princes Street, the city's main shopping street, and to provide easy access to Waverley Station.

Designed on two levels, it offers gaiety, colour and fun, with large and small speciality shops, wheelbarrow stalls with multi-coloured umbrellas, a food court, a wine bar and an open-air restaurant (with 350 seats). Cascading water, trees and bushes combine with mirrored surfaces and bright colours to make this a fun place.

Built in 1984.

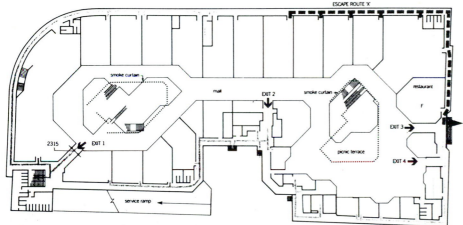

2

1 General view
2 Floor plan
3 Aerial view
4 Section

3

4

1

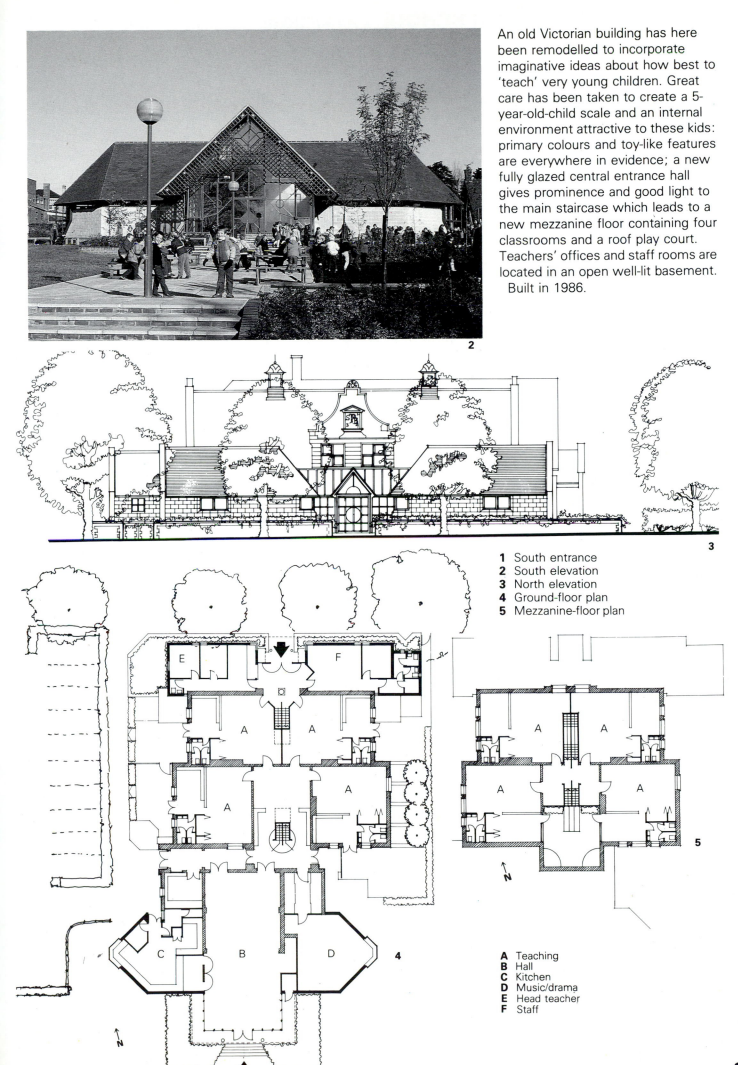

An old Victorian building has here been remodelled to incorporate imaginative ideas about how best to 'teach' very young children. Great care has been taken to create a 5-year-old-child scale and an internal environment attractive to these kids: primary colours and toy-like features are everywhere in evidence; a new fully glazed central entrance hall gives prominence and good light to the main staircase which leads to a new mezzanine floor containing four classrooms and a roof play court. Teachers' offices and staff rooms are located in an open well-lit basement.

Built in 1986.

1 South entrance
2 South elevation
3 North elevation
4 Ground-floor plan
5 Mezzanine-floor plan

A Teaching
B Hall
C Kitchen
D Music/drama
E Head teacher
F Staff

# BISHOPSTOKE INFANTS SCHOOL • HAMPSHIRE

COLIN STANSFIELD SMITH (Hampshire County Architect)

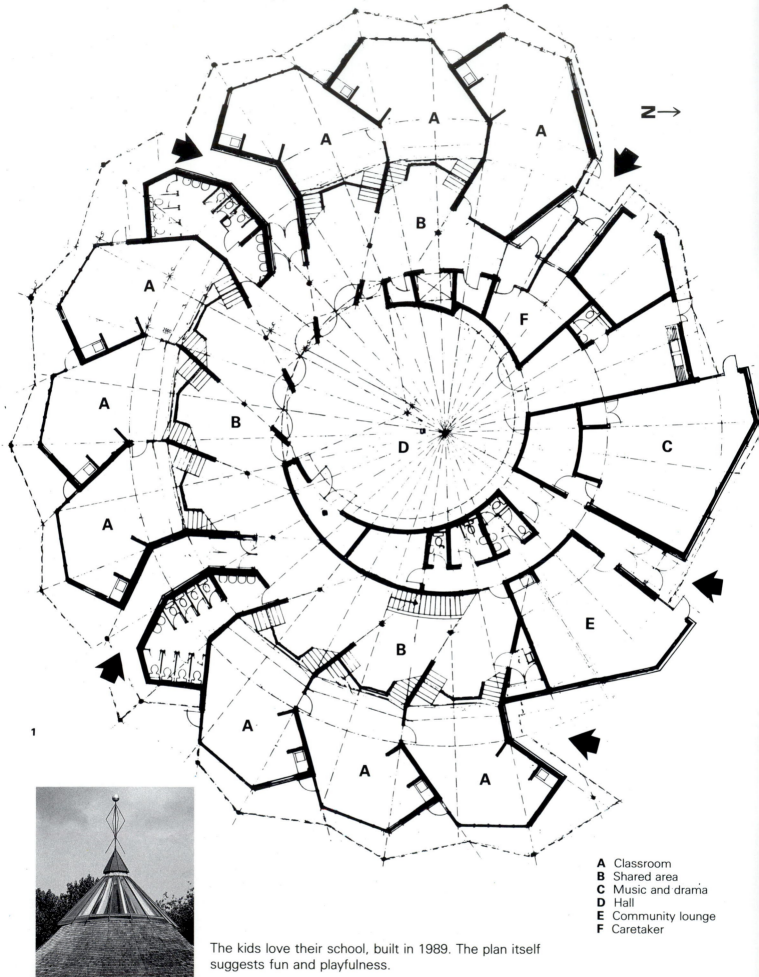

**N→**

A  Classroom
B  Shared area
C  Music and drama
D  Hall
E  Community lounge
F  Caretaker

The kids love their school, built in 1989. The plan itself
suggests fun and playfulness.

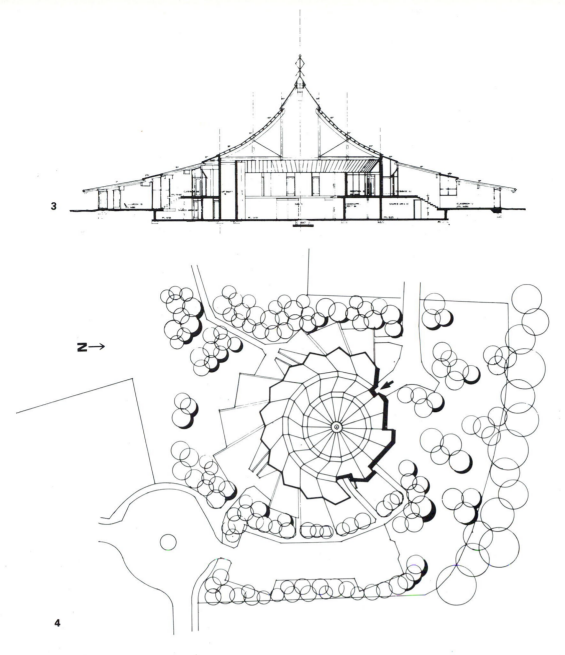

3

Z→

4

The lofty roof of this school will form a focal point within the community and become a source of visual excitement. The continuous bands of roof glazing light classrooms and shared areas which face south, with ramps and stairs down a half level to the shared area and hall, and up a half level to the class bases and administration rooms.

Walls are of loadbearing painted blockwork. Roof rafters and purlins are all exposed internally.

The school was opened in 1989.

1 Ground-floor plan (opposite)
2 The school's 'lofty roof'
3 Section
4 Site plan
5 Central hall
6 General view of school

5

6

# BRENTFORD LEISURE CENTRE • LONDON
## BOROUGH ARCHITECT PETER McKAY

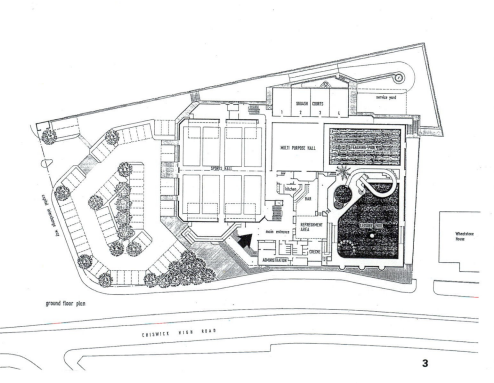

This multi-purpose centre of sport and leisure has been designed for all age groups in the Chiswick region of west London.

The main feature of the building is a large 'leisure pool' connected by a dramatic cantilevered slide-serpent to a smaller young children's pool and to a teaching pool. The decorative impact of the bright turquoise slide-serpent is increased by its constantly moving reflection in the water. Strong colour throughout the building plays an important role in the design.

The load-bearing concrete-block walls support light steel trusses and glazed roof, with a 50-m span. The roof glazing has been designed to give a diffused light to the whole pool area and to the sports hall and, at the same time, to prevent condensation.

The leisure centre was built in 1986.

1 The two pools
2 The sports hall
3 Layout plan

# NOAH'S ARK RESTAURANT • SAPPORO • JAPAN
## BRANSON COATES ARCHITECTURE

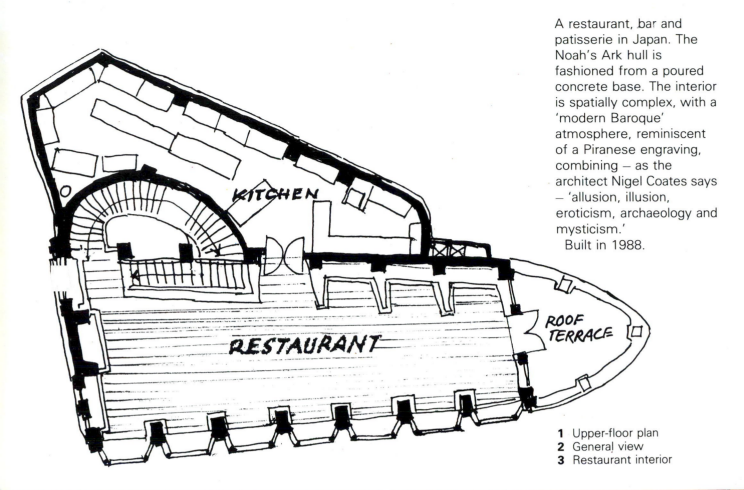

A restaurant, bar and patisserie in Japan. The Noah's Ark hull is fashioned from a poured concrete base. The interior is spatially complex, with a 'modern Baroque' atmosphere, reminiscent of a Piranese engraving, combining – as the architect Nigel Coates says – 'allusion, illusion, eroticism, archaeology and mysticism.'

Built in 1988.

**1** Upper-floor plan
**2** General view
**3** Restaurant interior

2

3

# 8 REFURBISHMENT

This country has many splendid examples of well-loved old buildings of character and real quality. With the passage of time the original use for which they were designed has changed so much that many of them no longer function satisfactorily. To avoid demolition they must be radically altered. One thinks of the Covent Garden opera house, the Old Vic theatre, the Whitechapel art gallery.

Because these buildings are so well-liked by so many people it needs special qualities in the architect to produce a design which will satisfy both the public and the professionals – sensitivity, skill, patience, determination, persistence and an ability to cooperate with all sorts of people. Jeremy Dixon's struggle to adapt the Covent Garden opera house to the needs of modern opera and to relate it to Inigo Jones' idea of a Renaissance urban square continues year after year. The danger is of course that a compromise solution to the problem presented to the architect will eventually be agreed and that will please nobody – least of all the architect.

Covent Garden market building, London

# HOUSE OF LORDS' CEILING • WESTMINSTER • LONDON

## DONALD INSALL & AILWYN BEST

1

3

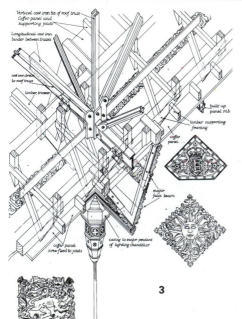

2

The Chamber of the House of Lords, in the Palace of Westminster, was completed in 1847 to designs by Sir Charles Barry, and was richly detailed by Augustus Pugin, appointed as Superintendent of wood-carving. By 1980 the great timber ceiling was in an advanced state of degradation, largely due to the heat of earlier gas-lighting. With great care and sensitivity the architects, acting on behalf of the Property Services Agency, have conserved and consolidated carved work, replaced damaged timbers, and have largely reconstructed the ceiling, incorporating a maximum of original craftsmanship. The work was completed for the State Opening of Parliament by HM the Queen in 1984.

1  The restored ceiling
2  Axonometric of roof construction
3  Details of ceiling and roof construction

140

# WATER TOWER FLATS • SOUTHALL • WEST LONDON

## FRANK VICKERY & ALINA MOFFETT

1

2

The architects converted this tall Victorian brick water-tower, which remained empty for many years, for a local cooperative community with a trade and professional membership (including Frank Vickery). Several members of the community – bricklayers, carpenters and others – were employed by the building contractor. The huge welded tank was removed and six floors of single-person bed-sitter flats and three-bedroom (shared) flats provided.

A mezzanine floor was added to the very high ground floor which provides a restaurant, community hall, gymnasium, study and laundry.

The only change made to the exterior of the building was the enlarging of the windows, in accordance with London's housing standards. The building in fact remains a Victorian landmark.

Refurbishment was completed in 1984.

1 General view
2 Typical elevation
3 A typical floor plan

a A three-persons shared flat
b A one-person flat

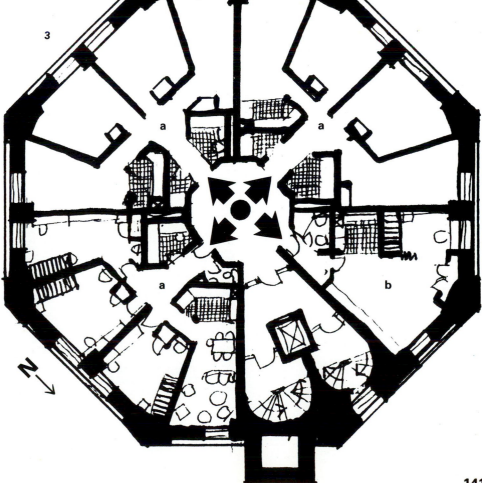

3

# ROYAL OPERA HOUSE EXTENSIONS • COVENT GARDEN • LONDON
## JEREMY DIXON (BDP) WITH EDWARD JONES

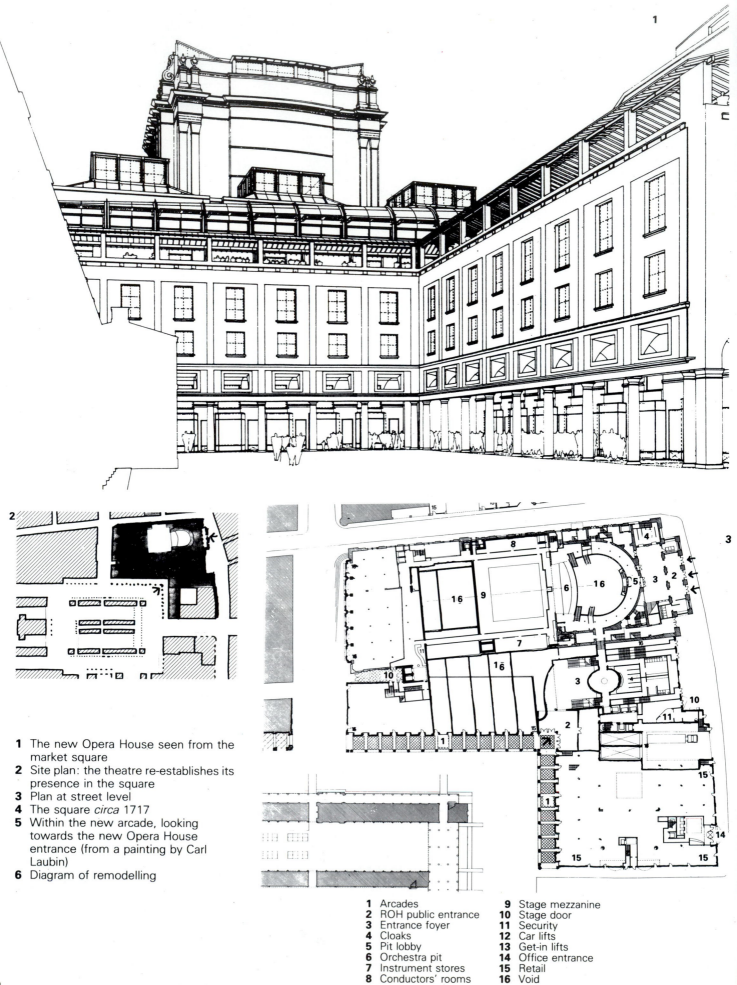

1 The new Opera House seen from the market square

2 Site plan: the theatre re-establishes its presence in the square

3 Plan at street level

4 The square *circa* 1717

5 Within the new arcade, looking towards the new Opera House entrance (from a painting by Carl Laubin)

6 Diagram of remodelling

| | | | |
|---|---|---|---|
| **1** | Arcades | **9** | Stage mezzanine |
| **2** | ROH public entrance | **10** | Stage door |
| **3** | Entrance foyer | **11** | Security |
| **4** | Cloaks | **12** | Car lifts |
| **5** | Pit lobby | **13** | Get-in lifts |
| **6** | Orchestra pit | **14** | Office entrance |
| **7** | Instrument stores | **15** | Retail |
| **8** | Conductors' rooms | **16** | Void |

4

5

The architects have here solved — with rare ingenuity and skill — an exceptionally difficult problem: to meet all the complex expansion requirements of the Royal Opera House (designed in 1858 by E.M. Barry) and at the same time to find an architectural approach that can respond to the diversity of the site context, bounded on the one hand by the implied formality of the Market Square (designed in 1631 by Inigo Jones), and on the other by a series of typical Covent Garden streets with their *ad hoc* accumulation of uses and architectural styles.

The new accommodation embraces two sides of the square and forms a strong link between the different departments of the two internationally renowned companies — the Royal Opera and the Royal Ballet.

The great new arcade is designed to recall Inigo Jones' original one; it unites the theatre and the Market Square; it is both a grand gallery leading to a new Opera House entrance from the square and an elegant shopping frontage opening on to the square.

After much discussion and delay the design was finally approved in September 1991.

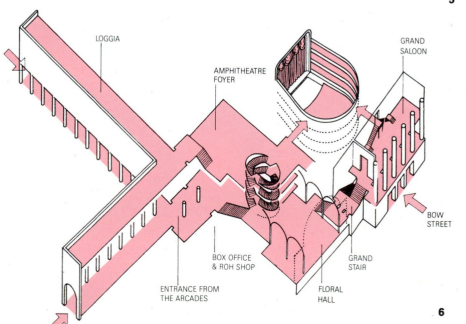

LOGGIA

AMPHITHEATRE FOYER

GRAND SALOON

BOX OFFICE & ROH SHOP

ENTRANCE FROM THE ARCADES

GRAND STAIR

FLORAL HALL

BOW STREET

6

# THE LIJNBAAN • ROTTERDAM • NETHERLANDS

## DEREK WALKER ASSOCIATES

1

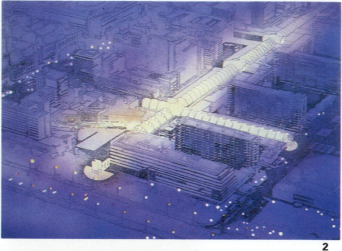

2

LIJNBAAN

3

Professor Derek Walker, with the Conran Design Group, has prepared a strategy for the radical reconstruction of one of Rotterdam's main central thoroughfares. When it opened for business in 1953 – rebuilt after its destruction in the war – it was hailed both as a symbol of the rebirth of a war-devastated city and as a breakthrough in shopping centre design. But it fell on hard times as retailers fled to the suburbs in pursuit of their customers and – as stores became larger – access to them, parking and servicing became increasingly difficult.

The reconstruction strategy underlines the street's traditional role as a speciality shopping centre, encourages continuous pedestrian circulation at first-floor level and allocates some areas for shows and live entertainment, fashion and apparel displays, with restaurant and bars and 'a children's world'. Most important of all, perhaps, the street is given a new attractive colourful image, with a lightweight translucent roof and passive climate control.

Work is expected to start in 1995.

1 Aerial view of street as existing
2 Aerial view of street as planned
3 New entrance to street
4 Perspective looking west
5 Cross-section
6 Longitudinal section
7 Upper-floor plan

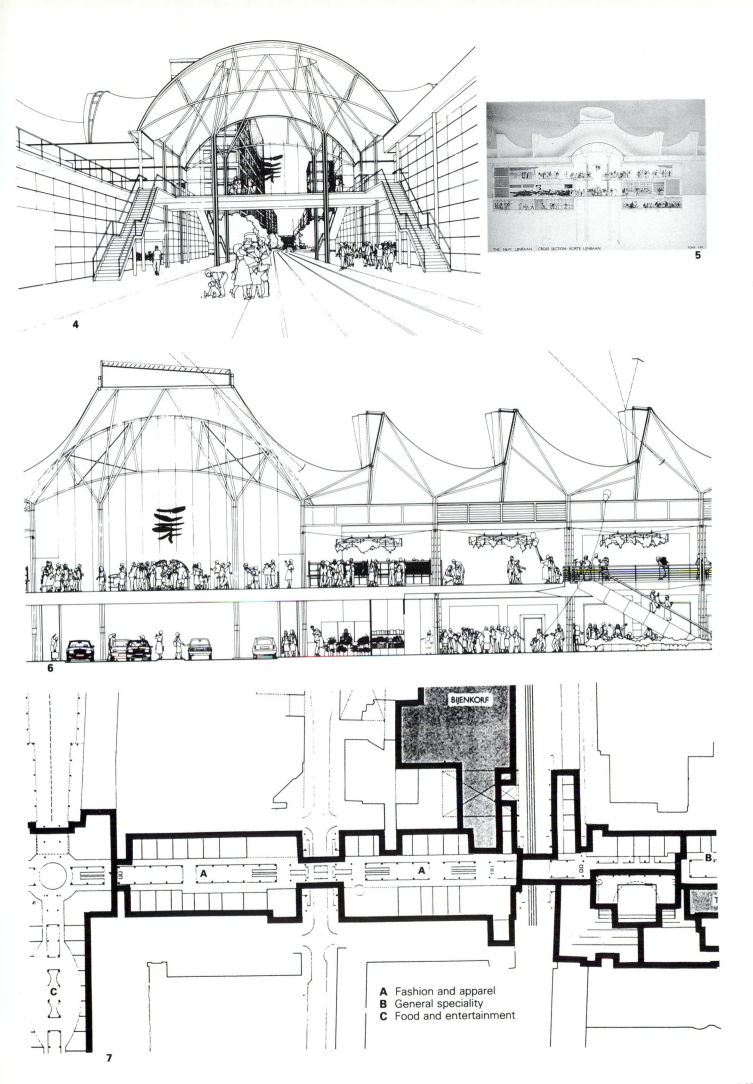

THE NEW LIJNBAAN : CROSS SECTION - KORTE LIJNBAAN

5

**A** Fashion and apparel
**B** General speciality
**C** Food and entertainment

BIJENKORF

# METROPOLIS RECORDING STUDIOS • CHISWICK • WEST LONDON
## POWELL-TUCK CONNOR & OREFELT

1

3

The design concept for these very successful recording studios was of 'a building within a building' – an old listed power station built in 1901. In a strongly modelled, almost dithyrambic composition, the architects have provided three main studios with private reception areas, two further mixing suites, a restaurant and bar, and administration and maintenance offices. The penthouse flats have been retained and proper access to them provided. One appreciative newspaper critic found that here 'imagination has been used to create architecture out of acoustics.'

Concrete and metal have been used externally to reflect the toughness of the original interior and because the density of concrete is important for acoustic separation. Internally the studios are well lit and their warmth glows into the colder, more aggressive atrium space. It must be satisfying to the architects to know that musicians who have recorded here have given the design high praise.

The studios opened in 1990.

2

4

1 A typical studio
2 Central atrium
3 General view of building
4 Another view of the atrium
5 Architects' sketch of central area
6 Ground-floor plan
7 Upper-floor plan

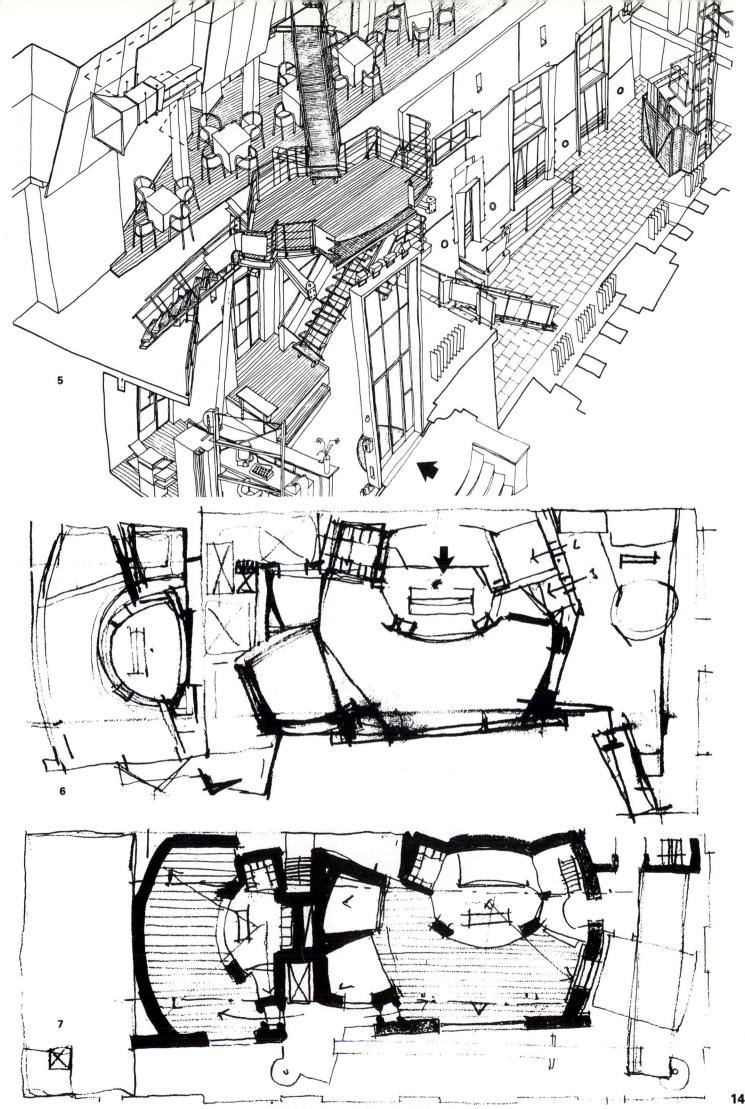

5

6

7

# IMAGINATION DESIGN'S HQ BUILDING • BLOOMSBURY • LONDON
## RON HERRON ASSOCIATES

1

'. . . in fact the refurbishment shows how essentially practical the technological superhumanism of the Archigram era really was.' (Martin Pauley writing in the *Architectural Review*).

Ron Herron was of course one of the Archigram group and here, in converting two 90-year-old buildings and the open space between them into the headquarters building of the Imagination design firm, he has demonstrated the truth of Pawley's statement.

The curved front wall of the old school building has been retained in its original state; all other walls have been painted white (inside and out); and the central open space has been converted into an atrium by floating a tent-like translucent PVC roof over it, with a series of lightweight steel and aluminium gangways criss-crossing it at different levels and different angles. The PVC roof also passes over the lower block to form a new exhibition and presentation space giving on to a south-facing covered balcony.

Built in 1989.

2

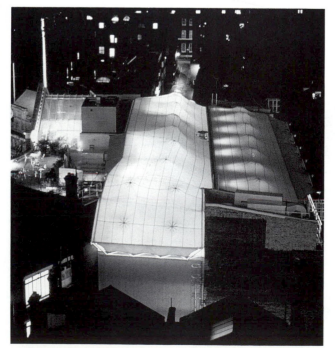

3

1 Roof
2 Elevation
3 Roof
4 Section
5 Atrium
6 Second-floor plan

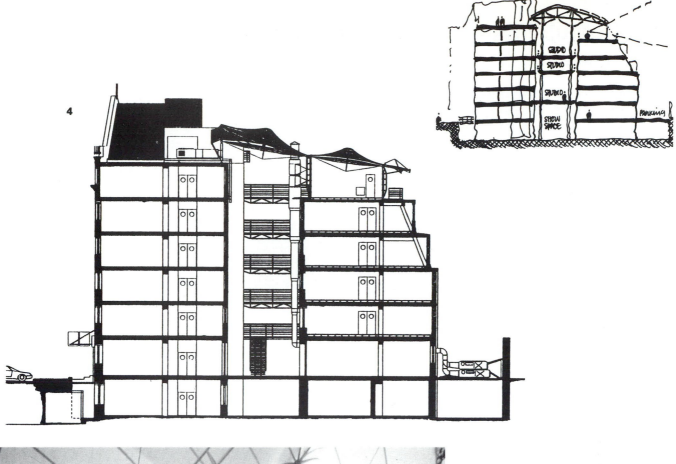

4

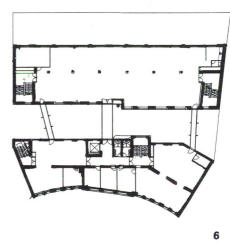

6

5

# DESIGN MUSEUM • SOUTH-EAST LONDON
## CONRAN ROCHE

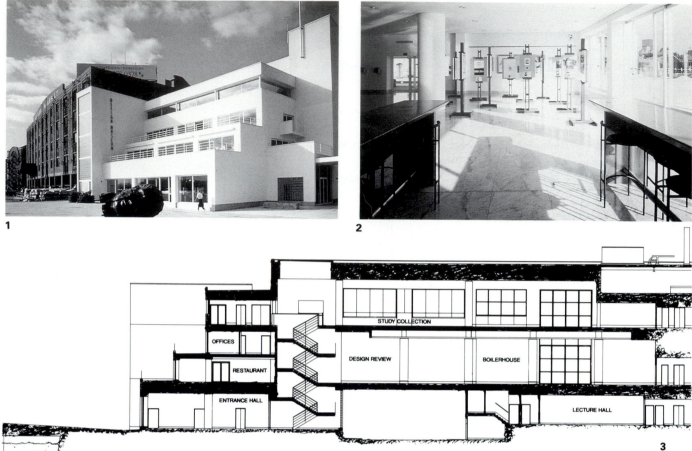

1

2

3

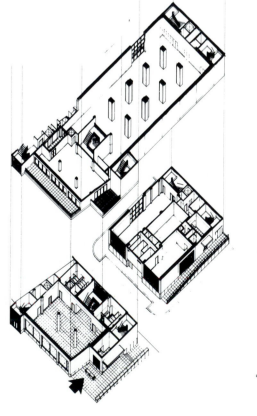

4

5

Conran Roche have sensitively converted a 1960s concrete and brick warehouse overlooking the River Thames into a design museum, with two double-height exhibition galleries, a spacious entrance foyer, library, lecture theatre, restaurant and staff offices. The very light colours of the building – internally and externally – add a welcome touch of elegance to this rather dreary stretch of the River Thames and give a good background to the display of well-designed objects and artefacts.

The museum opened in 1988.

1 General view from the river
2 Exhibition gallery interior
3 Section
4 Ground- and first-floor plans
5 Site plan

# WHITECHAPEL ART GALLERY • EAST LONDON
## COLQUHOUN & MILLER

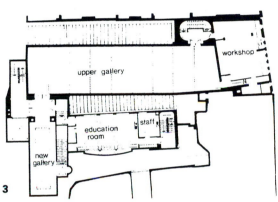

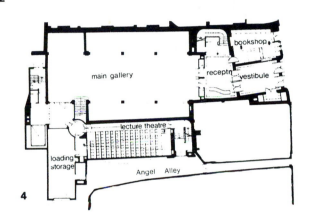

1 Entrance elevation
2 Upper gallery
3 Upper-floor plan
4 Ground-floor plan
5 Cross-section

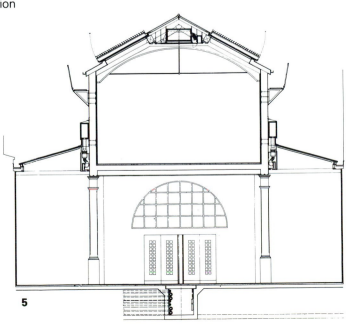

Colin Davies, in the *Architects' Journal* of October 1985, wrote as follows:

**'The Whitechapel Art Gallery had a remarkable façade when it was completed in 1901 to the design of C. Harrison Townsend, but a very cramped, though functional, interior. Colquhoun and Miller, in the remodelling of the gallery, have redressed the balance and given the building an interior that integrates the best of the Townsend interiors with a series of new spaces.'**

The removal of the existing staircase makes the main gallery clearly visible from the entrance lobby and a new staircase leads from this gallery to those on the upper floor.

The Gallery was reopened in 1985.

# MARITIME MUSEUM • BARROW-IN-FURNESS • CUMBRIA
## CRAIG & GREEN

1

2

A delightful conversion of a disused Victorian graving dock at Barrow-in-Furness (Cumbria) into a maritime museum. The architects have used the powerful character of the old sandstone and steel amphitheatre to create a multi-level display of maritime engineering and the artefacts associated with it.

The new museum symbolizes the revitalization of Barrow-in-Furness as a major centre of ship-building. It was opened in 1990.

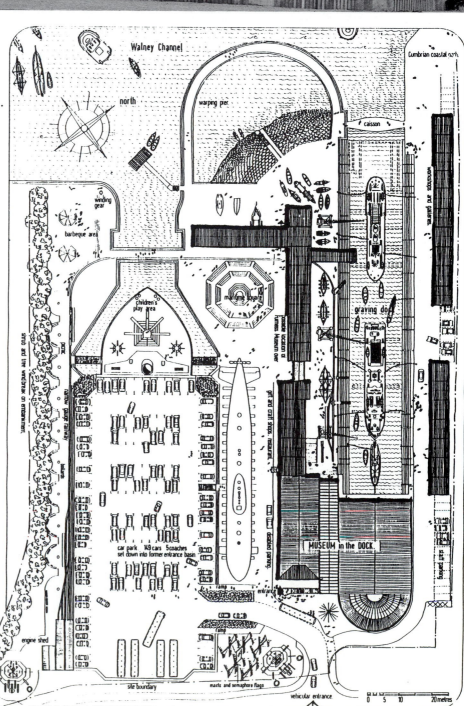

3

# CROWNDALE COMMUNITY CENTRE • CAMDEN • NORTH LONDON
## ROCK TOWNSEND

1

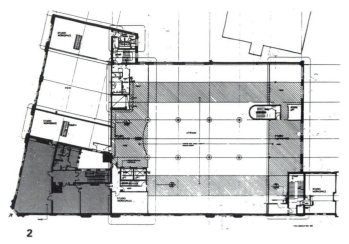

2

1 General view of building
2 Ground-floor plan
3 Atrium

A very successful creation of a north London community centre by converting a well-loved landmark building and adding a new one alongside it.

The centre functions as a working community – a collaboration between individual and independent enterprises sharing common support facilities and shared services such as conference rooms, exhibition space, crèche, reception, security and a health centre.

This is a building where no one use dominates; its fulcrum is the old light well which, with its new roof, has become a four-storey atrium entered from the 'public' areas: shops, restaurant, café, reception and main concourse. It opened in 1990.

3

# HOSPITALS FOR SICK CHILDREN • CENTRAL LONDON

## POWELL MOYA PARTNERSHIP

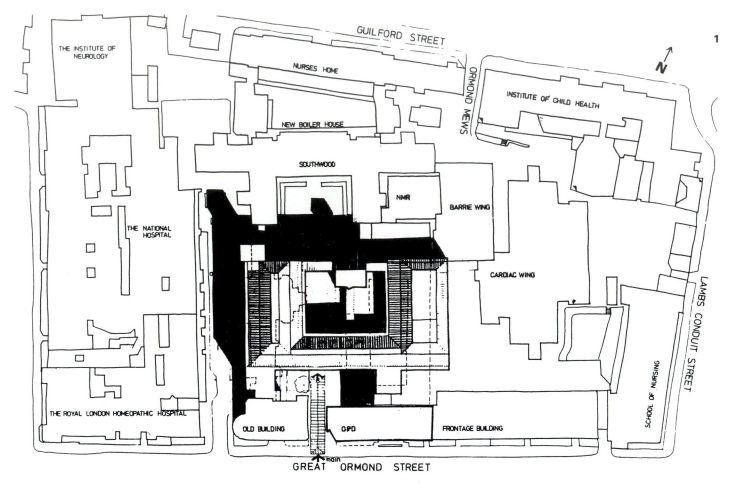

1. Site plan of hospitals
2. Elevation detail
3. Aerial view of model
4. Hospital chapel
5. New entrance from Great Ormond Street
6. New outpatients waiting area

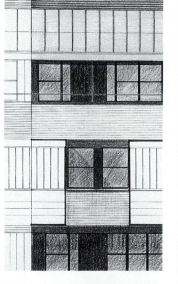

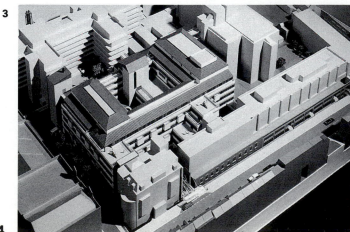

The Great Ormond Street Hospitals for Sick Children desperately needed modernization and redevelopment within the core of their central London site. The key to the 'town plan' of the whole hospital complex, old and new, is a new spine of 'streets' – broad naturally-lit corridors at each level – running east–west along the centre of the site.

The new wards consist mainly of single rooms for child and parent, with private bathrooms. There will also be six new operating theatres, a 30-bed intensive therapy unit, and extended outpatients department and underground car parking. The fine chapel (built in 1875) stood in the way of redevelopment; it has been carefully moved and will become an integral part of the remodelled hospitals. Construction: steel frame; external pale yellow brickwork, with dark blue horizontal bands.

The extensive remodelling of the hospital complex started in the mid-1980s. The new outpatients department (OPD) opened in 1990.

5

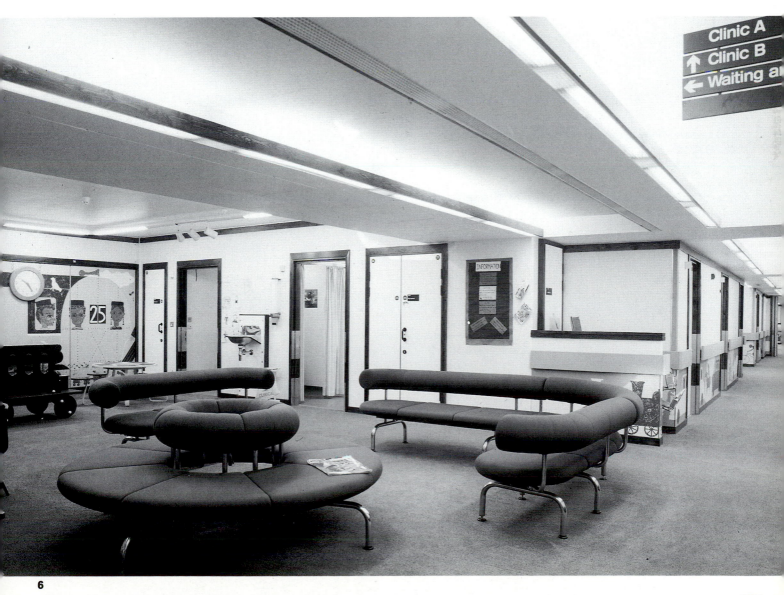

6

# ST PANCRAS STATION HOTEL • LONDON
## YRM ARCHITECTS

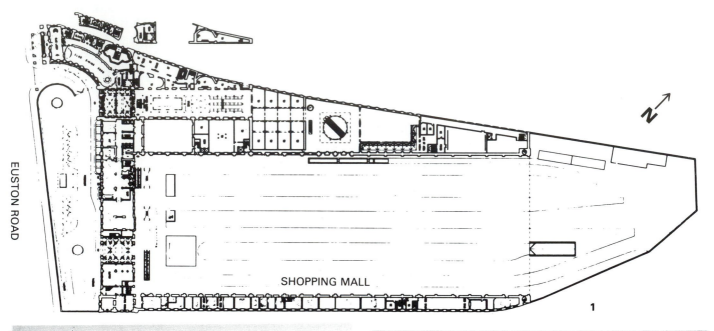

EUSTON ROAD

SHOPPING MALL

1

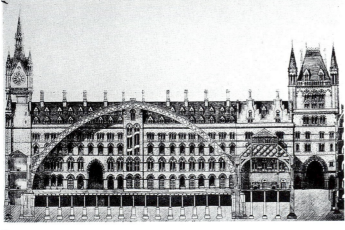

2

3

One of the most difficult of refurbishment problems: how to adapt Sir George Gilbert Scott's ornate neo-Gothic Victorian masterpiece for modern living without losing the sense of grandeur and splendour of the original.

YRM have achieved just that by retaining the huge brick arches, cast-iron trusses and high ceilings, but harnessing modern technology to give functional workability and comfort to these impressive spaces.

On a more intimate scale, each of the 127 five-star bedrooms in the hotel has a fine four-poster bed (with Victorian draperies and tassles) and a mock Adam fireplace.

Project designed in the late 1980s; work on site expected to start in the mid-1990s.

**1** Ground-floor plan
**2** East elevation (to the station)
**3** A typical bedroom
**4** Brasserie (the former booking hall)

4

# 9
# PARTICIPATION

The self-build do-it-yourself movement has been growing steadily in Britain for the past decade. We have now a considerable number of housing associations and cooperative societies dedicated to helping people to build their own homes themselves. Some architects act as professional advisers to these groups, sometimes representing them at public enquiries and at negotiations with the local authority and with central government. Architect Rod Hackney (RIBA President in 1988) has pioneered this work in the Midlands, and some boroughs – in London and elsewhere – are now working closely with such groups.

Walter Segal developed a system of easily assembled lightweight timber construction which people could readily understand and use in building their own houses. Today Jon Broome advises many self-builders on the use of the Segal system on various sites in the London borough of Lewisham.

The RIBA is the headquarters of what has become known as the Community Architecture movement. It is expanding steadily and many architects, as well as the general public, believe that it will continue to grow in strength and national importance.

# SELF-BUILD HOUSES • LEWISHAM • SOUTH LONDON
## WALTER SEGAL & JON BROOME

**1**   **2**

**3**

A self-build timber housing system was designed by architect Walter Segal in 1962 and a few prototype houses were built. In the mid-1980s the London borough of Lewisham adopted the system and encouraged local people to use it in building their own houses on five or six different sites in the borough.

The construction method of posts, beams and panels is basically simple and easy to use, and offers a large number of different floor plans – giving the self-builder a big choice.

The architect's team advises the amateur builders on technical and legal matters and encourages them to produce their own drawings to illustrate their personal requirements.

Work started at Lewisham in the early 1980s.

**4**

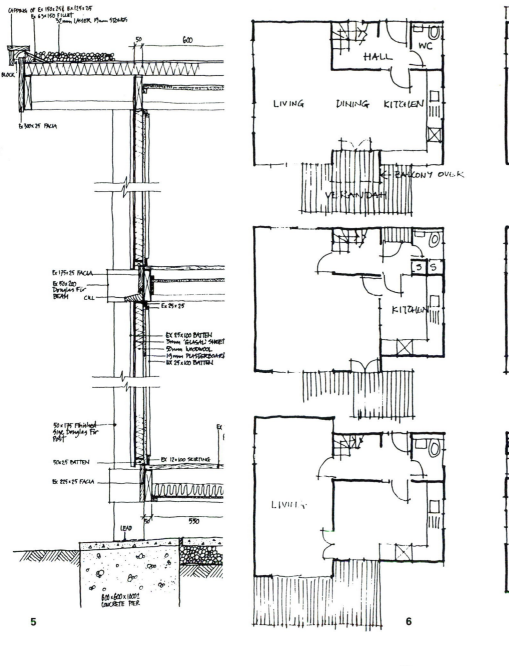

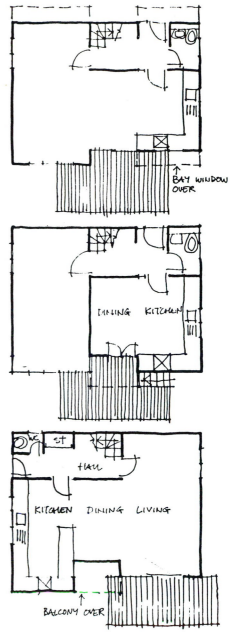

**5**

**6**

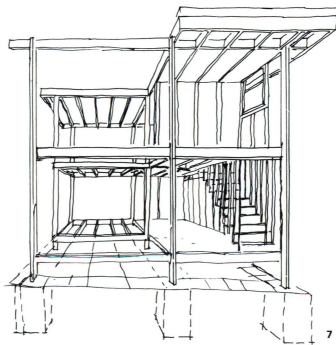

**7**

1 A two-storey house
2 House under construction
3 A typical bungalow
4 A typical interior
5 Two-storey wall section
6 Six of many possible floor
  plans
7 Timber structure

Labels on section (5):

CAPPING OF Ex 150x25 & Ex 125x25
Ex 63x150 FILLET
32mm LAYER 19mm STONES
50  600
BLOCK
Ex 300x25 FACIA
Ex 175x25 FACIA
Ex 50x200 Douglas Fir BEAM
CILL
Ex 25x25
EX 25x100 BATTEN
3mm 'GLASAL' SHEET
50mm WOODWOOL
19mm PLASTERBOARD
EX 25x100 BATTEN
50x175 Finished Size Douglas Fir Post
50x25 BATTEN
EX 12x100 SKIRTING
Ex 225x25 FACIA
LEAD
50  550
600 x 600 x 1000? CONCRETE PIER

Labels on floor plans (6):

HALL  WC
LIVING  DINING  KITCHEN
BALCONY OVER
VERANDAH
BAY WINDOW OVER
KITCHEN
DINING  KITCHEN
LIVING
WC  st
HALL
KITCHEN  DINING  LIVING
BALCONY OVER

# SELF-BUILD HOUSING • MACCLESFIELD • CHESHIRE
## ROD HACKNEY

3

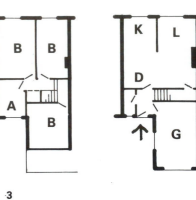

One of the first community-participation self-build housing schemes was started in Macclesfield by architect Rod Hackney who acted as 'professional adviser' on design to each house builder and represented them in negotiations with the local authority and with central government.

Each house was basically designed and financed by the individual owner–occupier.

Building began in 1984.

2

1 A typical housing court
2 Duplex flats at Roan House Way
3 House floor plans
4 The Prince of Wales chatting with self-builders and the architect

# SINGLE-FAMILY HOUSE • HIGHGATE • NORTH LONDON

## JOHN WINTER & ASSOCIATES

The architect designed the shell of this house overlooking Highgate cemetery and with magnificent views of central London. The client designed and built everything else.

Partly because of poor soil conditions on the site and partly for fun the house is supported on one central column with the first floor trussed up as a two-way cantilever, using the full storey height as a structural member.

The house is remarkable for the strong and clear external expression of the structure.

Built in 1980.

**1** General view from cemetery
**2** Lower-floor plan
**3** Upper-floor plan

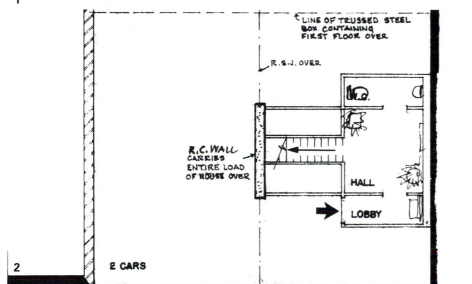

LINE OF TRUSSED STEEL BOX CONTAINING FIRST FLOOR OVER

R.S.J. OVER

R.C. WALL CARRIES ENTIRE LOAD OF HOUSE OVER

W.C.

HALL

LOBBY

2 CARS

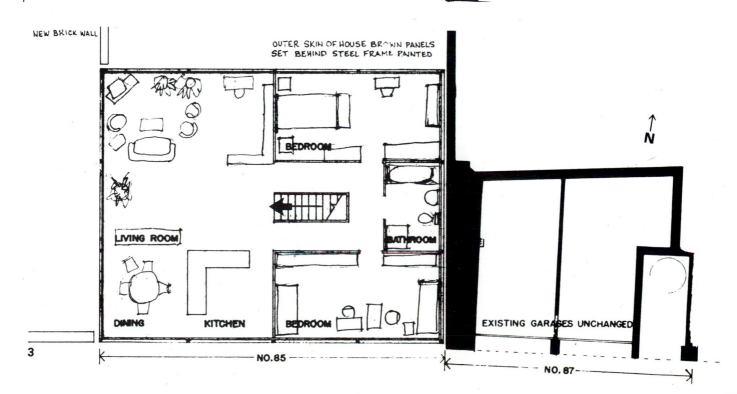

NEW BRICK WALL

OUTER SKIN OF HOUSE BROWN PANELS SET BEHIND STEEL FRAME PAINTED

BEDROOM

LIVING ROOM

BATHROOM

DINING   KITCHEN   BEDROOM

EXISTING GARAGES UNCHANGED

N

NO. 85

NO. 87

# COMMUNITY CENTRE • MORLEY COLLEGE • WESTMINSTER • LONDON
## JOHN WINTER & ASSOCIATES

1

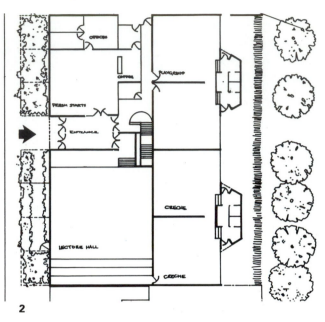

2

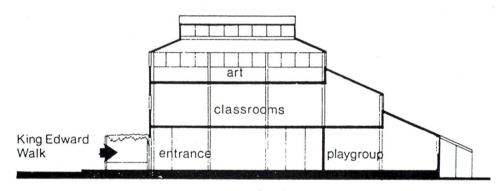

3

King Edward Walk

This is a good example of unusually close collaboration between client, architect and builder, enabling construction to go ahead almost without a brief and design decisions to be taken as the work proceeded. The building serves the local community, offering meeting rooms, crèches and classes in art, English and literacy. The building has a reinforced concrete frame.
  Built in 1983.

1 General view
2 Ground-floor plan
3 Section
4 Top floor (art room)
5 Site plan

4

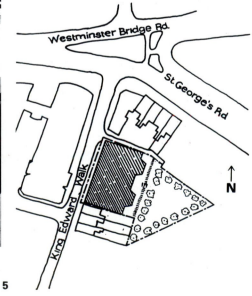

5

# ARTIST'S STUDIO • NETTLECOMBE • DEVON

DAVID LEA

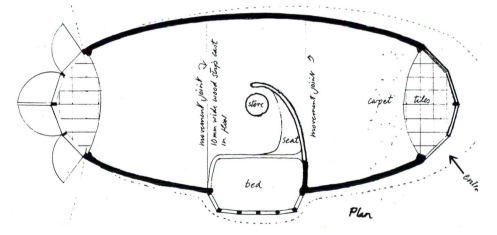

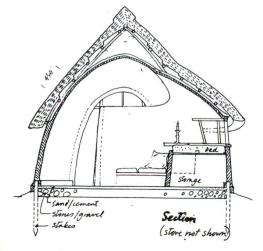

The architect's brief was that this studio should be cheap to construct, of local materials and simple enough to be built by the painter and her small family. Young elastic maple branches, in a criss-cross pattern, were used as the basic structure — stiffened by chicken wire netting, with straw in-filling, rendered inside and outside with cement plaster. The basket-like form has a thatched roof supported in the traditional way. The concrete floor is laid on consolidated earth and covered with a carpet.

The little studio has weathered very well and has already become an unobtrusive part of the rural landscape.

Built in 1984.

# ST MARY'S CHURCH • BARNES • WEST LONDON

## EDWARD CULLINAN, MARK BEEDLE & ALAN SHORT

1

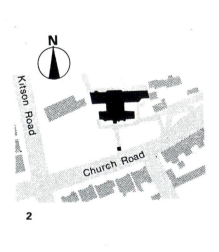

2

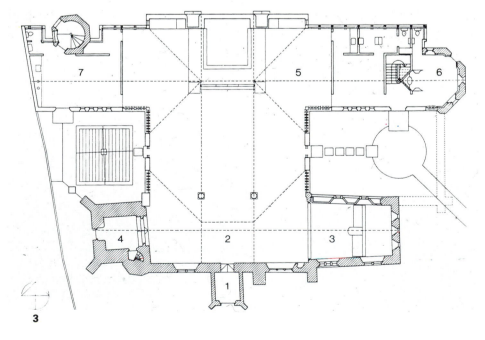

3

St Mary's church was destroyed by fire in 1978. As the tower, the south wall and a few fragments of other walls remained after the fire, it was decided to rebuild it. There followed five years of detailed discussions between architect, church committee and congregation. The result is a fine plan and an impressive church interior, with the new construction imaginatively and skilfully integrated with the old. The original mediaeval timber technology has been used — but in a new way — to create an atmosphere conducive to quiet contemplation and prayer.

The church was reopened in 1984.

**1** Church interior
**2** Site plan
**3** Plan
**4** Architects' preliminary discussion sketches
**5** Section
**6** Typical construction details

4

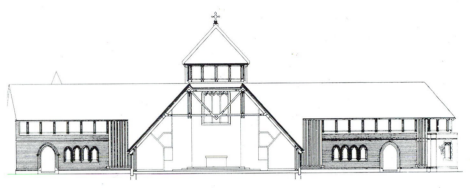

5

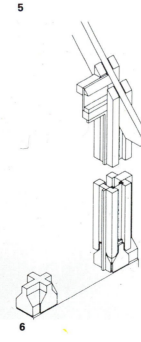

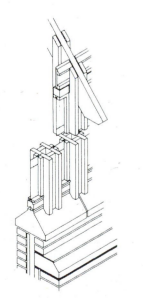

6

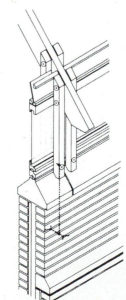

# 10
# DECONSTRUCTION

Ours is a violent age. One thinks of names like Chernobyl, Heysel, Lockerbie, Saddam Hussein. Alongside the violence there is disintegration, central city decay and dereliction, homelessness, despair; and milder words come to mind like indigestion, irrationality, illogicality, drug addiction.

Many artists are moved to express this tragic negative part of our society in their work. We think of Salvador Dali and the Surrealists, of Picasso's Guernica, and of the paintings of Francis Bacon.

Some architects feel the same way and so we have deconstruction. But architecture is a social art, and a positive rather than a negative one: function is important; a building must work. The American architect Peter Eisenman is generally considered to be the theorist of the deconstruction movement and many of his houses in the USA illustrate the theory of deconstruction well.

For me Bernard Tschumi's layout for Paris' new park at La Villette is a more convincing illustration of the theory. I visited it in 1989 and was fascinated by his 'folies' which are located at the intersection of his grid of upper-level pedestrian walkways. Each folly offers the visitor a different set of experiences, and he or she responds positively and with obvious enjoyment. Here is architecture almost without a purpose – except to fascinate; and the public responds by being fascinated. Here are twisted geometries all right – but indigestion? If most of the 19 follies at La Villette are to have a function other than to fascinate and intrigue, that other function will remain incidental. Here function

Cover of *Punch* magazine (20 May 1987)

follows form (the opposite to the Miesian dictum) and the form is a steel one – and first and foremost abstract – and painted bright red.

Peter Cook, Zaha Hadid and OMA (Elia Zenghelis and Rem Koolhaas) are busy designing some interesting Deconstructivist buildings, but, alas, all of them overseas and most of them not yet built. Hadid's prizewinning Peak Club in Hong Kong, on a steeply sloping site overlooking the city, is a splendid example of Deconstructivist thinking. She describes it like this:

'The Peak Club is a luxurious hedonistic merging of nature and the man-made in its combination of club facilities for the high-living and the creation of a new geology to replace the removed earth.'

Described as 'a horizontal skyscraper' the building consists of a layering of superimposed groups of accommodation set at different angles and creating positive spaces and voids between.

This layering and use of unexpected angles is typical of the attitude of British deconstruction architects. It is a dominant feature of the work of both Peter Cook and Elia Zenghelis in Germany. Another feature of their work is that it is invariably illustrated by splendid drawings – and sometimes by paintings.

A drawing by Zaha Hadid

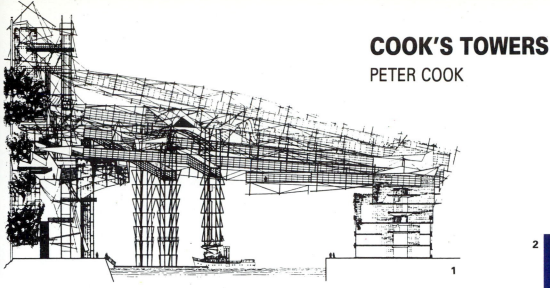

# COOK'S TOWERS

## PETER COOK

1 'Real city' Frankfurt
2 Paris exhibition
3 An early essay in
   deconstruction
4 The 'Wetterturm',
   Frankfurt

Professor Peter Cook has brilliantly applied the deconstruction ethic to the design of tower buildings (illustrated here by four of his beautiful drawings). His Frankfurt studio tower is not alas likely to be built, and his *tour aux maisons tournantes et aux jardins verticaux* – for a site at the pont de Bercy in Paris – was shown at the 1989 Paris exhibition of 21st-century ideas.

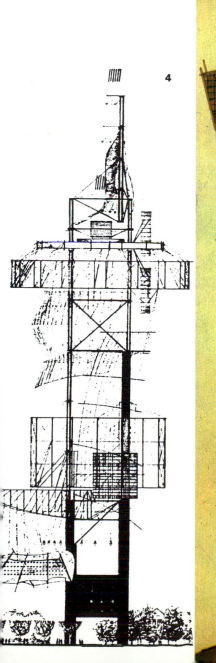

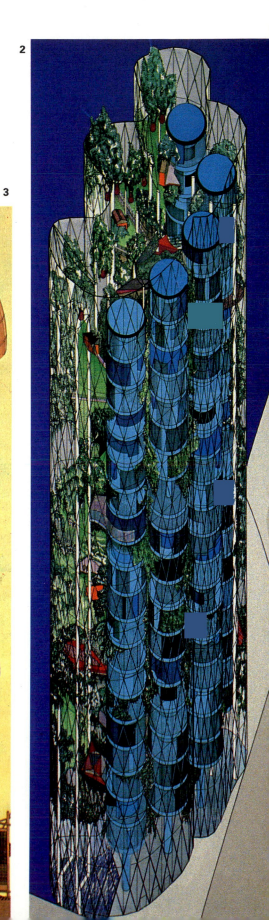

# TOKYO PAVILION (THE TOMIGAYA PROJECT)

ZAHA HADID

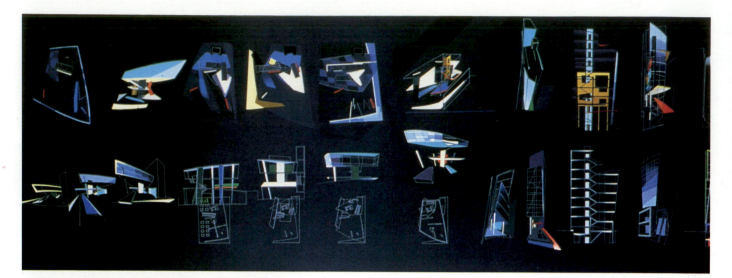

1

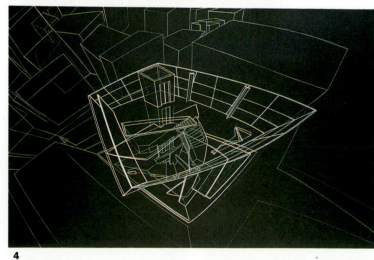

2

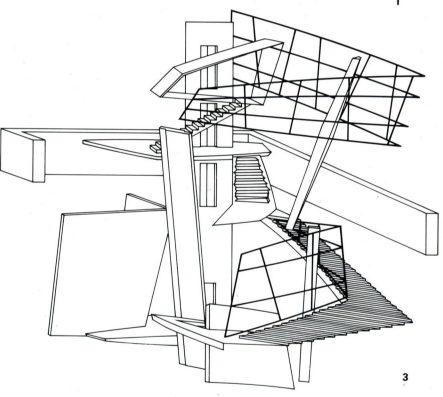

3

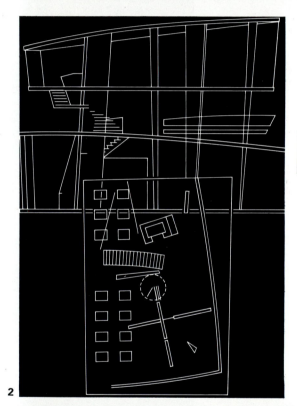

4

The site for this pavilion is a square (12 × 15 m) in one of Tokyo's cluttered residential neighbourhoods. The building is a series of suspended horizontal spaces and vertical elements 'interlocked by the spiralling motion of stairs and cantilevered platforms' – a concrete and glass structure that floats above the open ground floor. The basement is a strong volume, with sloping walls and gently curved ceiling which allows light to filter down.
   Built in 1992.

1 Studies for two Tokyo projects
2 Section and plan superimposed
3 Circulation elements
4 View through the pavilion towards the basement

# MOONSOON RESTAURANT • SAPPORO • JAPAN

## ZAHA HADID

The Moonsoon restaurant interiors were obviously inspired by Zaha Hadid's successful Groningen pavilion in Holland which was essentially a box of deconstructivist ideas.

The Sapporo restaurant (1991) is also a box (of plastic materials) divided into sections, with strongly contrasting atmospheres: a 'land of fire' on the upper floor, with vivid red and yellow fibreglass forms which appear to float above the central bar; and a 'land of ice' on the lower floor, with quiet, more restrained pale green and grey cavernous forms, expertly crafted metal and glass fittings and detachable plug-in seat backs and table tops.

**1** Upper floor
**2** Section
**3** Lower floor

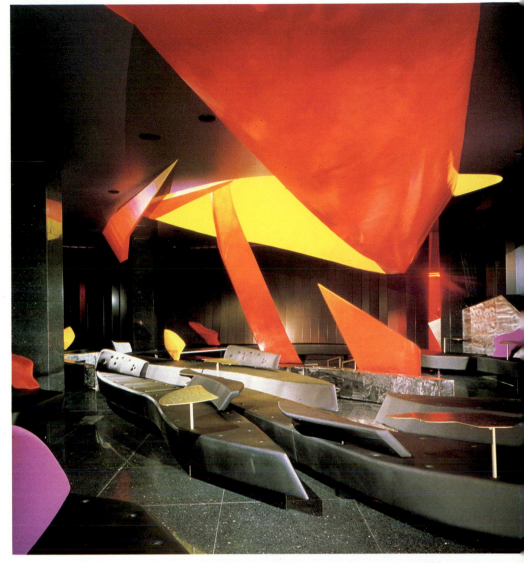

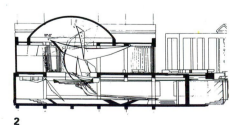

2

3

# STAINED GLASS MUSEUM • LANGEN • GERMANY

## PETER COOK & CHRISTINE HAWLEY

Cook and Hawley's elegant design demonstrates well the main characteristics of deconstruction. The design is dominated by ramps and stairs which give direct access to the upper-level galleries and offices and are dramatically juxtaposed with the main mass of building.

Designed in 1982 but not built.

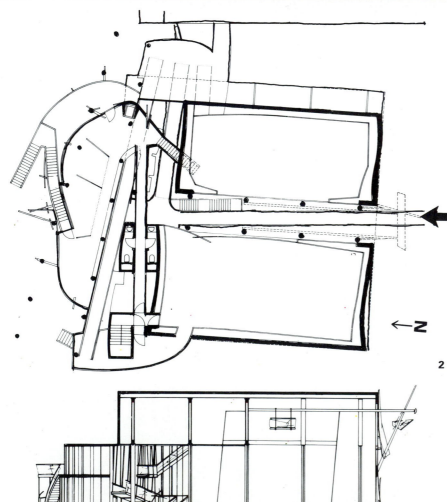

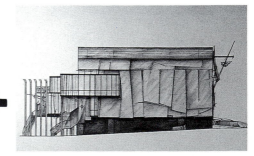

← N

1 Model
2 Ground-floor plan
3 Section
4 West elevation

# RESTAURANT/CANTEEN • FRANKFURT • GERMANY
## COOK & HAWLEY WITH ENGINEER KLAUS BOLINGER

The glazed roof of this little staff and students' restaurant/canteen at the Frankfurt Art Academy appears to float above an existing colonnade of classical columns to which it is actually attached by steel tension cables. The whole end of the roof intriguingly tilts up in hot weather.

Built in 1989.

**1**

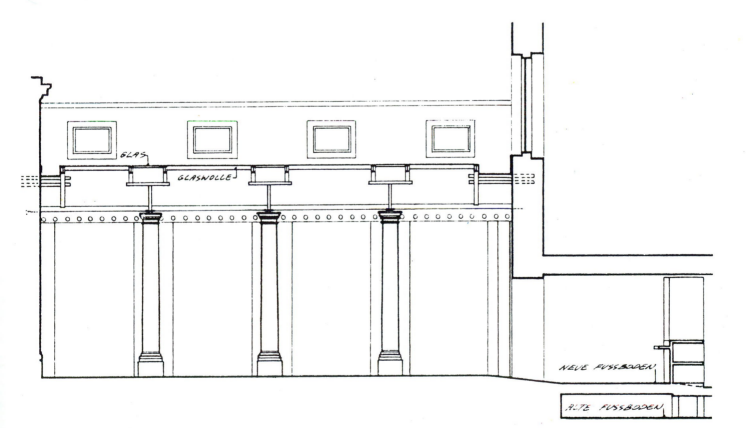

GLAS

GLASWOLLE

NEUE FUSSBODEN

ALTE FUSSBODEN

**2**

# 'LA SERRE' BUILDING • LA VILLETTE • PARIS • FRANCE

## CEDRIC PRICE

La Serre expresses the Deconstructivist ethic in three ways: the layering of the various public access features of the interior space; the two long walkways accessible to wheelchairs and set at different angles; and a central circular observation platform which appears to float in space.

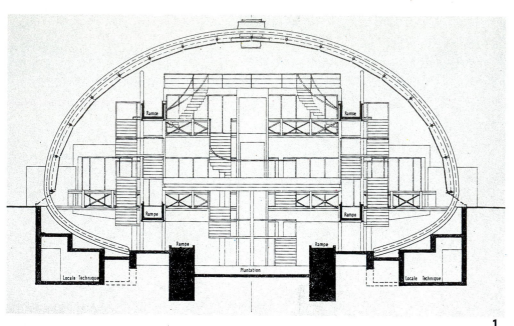

1

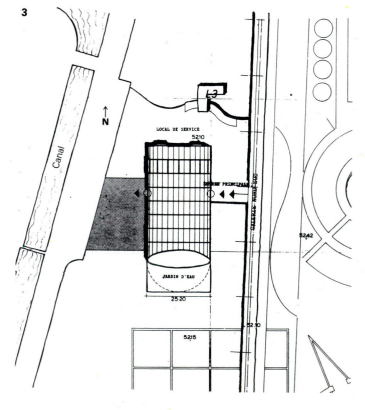

2

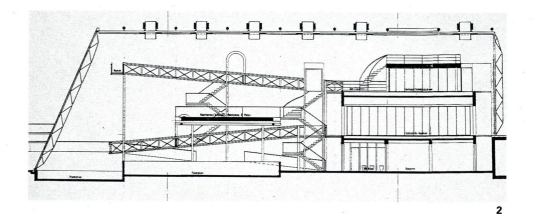

3

Cedric Price's glass building has two distinct activity zones: a habitable greenhouse where spectacular plants form a permanent setting for exhibitions and social events; and a series of volumes providing facilities for meetings, research, administration and servicing. The whole building is enriched by the scent, colours and textures of the varied plants. The public and invited guests are admitted both to the building and to its adjacent gardens.

The building is profiled partly below ground level to achieve a maximum clear internal height of 13 m. The glass skin (6 mm toughened obscured) is hung from the external main structure which consists of a series of transverse elliptical tubes, with tubular longitudinal purlins. Space frames (internal south, external north) support clear glazing on the end faces.

Work on site is expected to start in the mid-1990s.

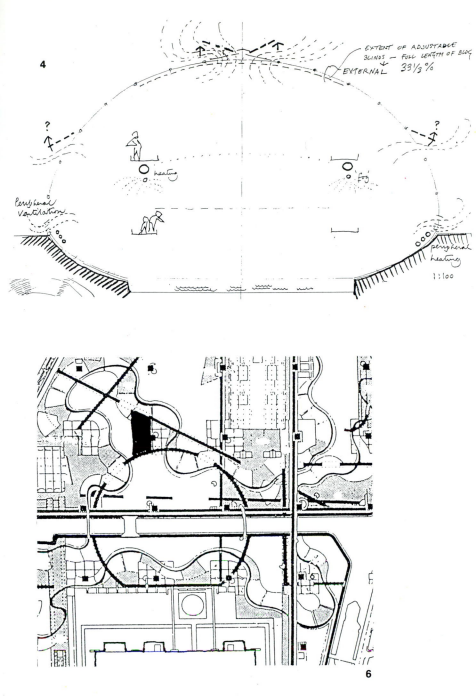

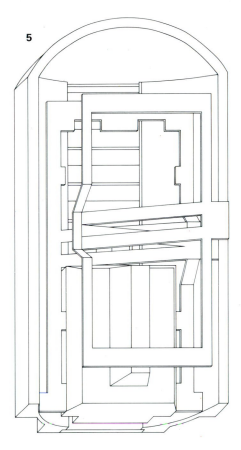

4

EXTENT OF ADJUSTABLE
BLINDS — FULL LENGTH OF BLDG
EXTERNAL 33⅓ %

5

6

1 Cross-section
2 Longitudinal section
3 Site plan
4 Architect's design sketch
5 View of model showing ramps
6 Part plan of La Villette park
7 Model: view from the south-east

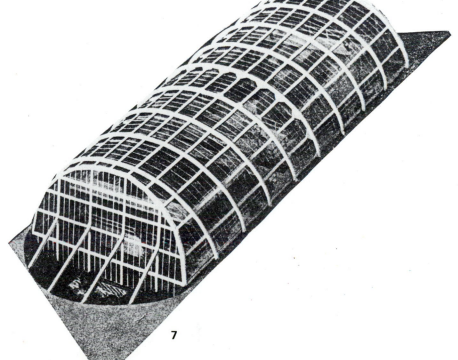

7

# LEGENDS NIGHTCLUB • CENTRAL LONDON
## EVA JIRICNA • ARCHITECT

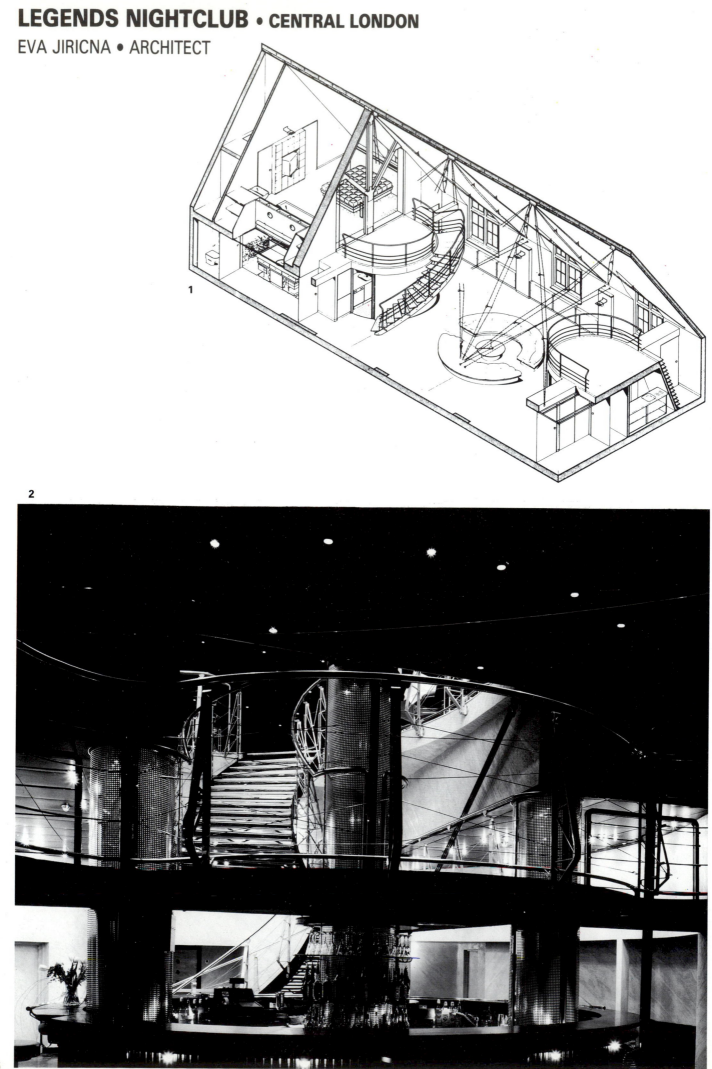

1

2

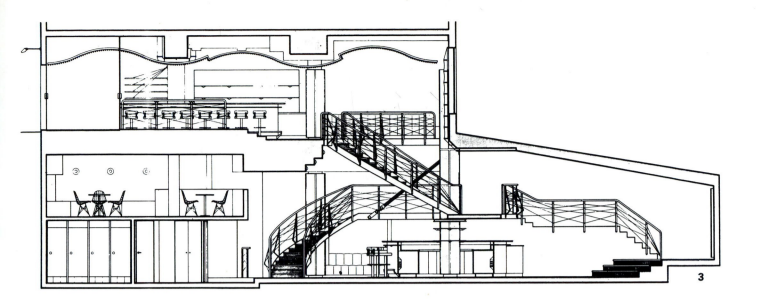

With skill and ingenuity the architects have here created a luxurious sophisticated night-club from rather a conventional rectangular space. Part of an upper floor has been removed to create an impressive full-height central area and a mezzanine floor added as a gallery overlooking it. The three levels thus created are joined together by curving staircases beautifully detailed and seeming to float in space. This is perhaps not a full-blooded example of Deconstructivist thinking, but nonetheless – with its use of curves, its free-standing balconies and galleries, and the dramatic placing of the three staircases – it expresses well the spirit of Deconstructivism.

The club was opened in 1987.

**1** Isometric drawing
**2** Part interior view
**3** Section
**4** Mezzanine-floor plan

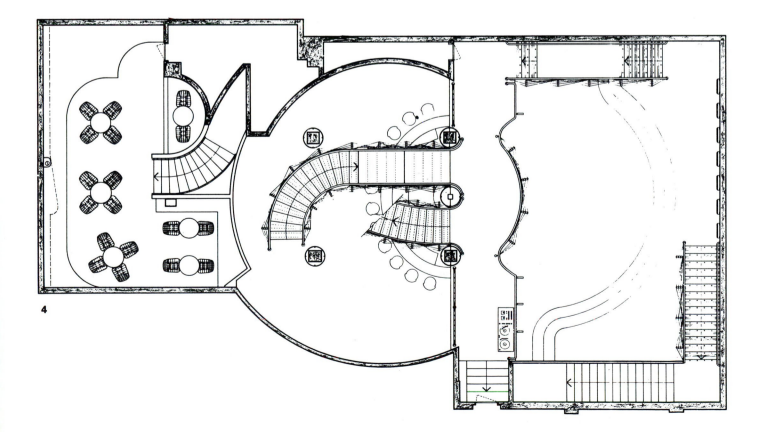

# THE FUTURE

'Jencks' four-seasons house is bewildering rather than satisfying.' The symbolic staircase.

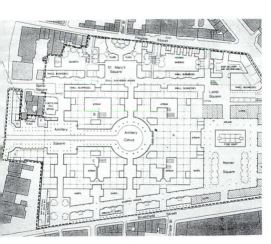

'...a rather rigid formality very different from the mediaeval street pattern [of London].' Spitalfields.

'...inflexibility of the Beaux-Arts tradition.' Greenwich.

### POST-MODERNISM

Those architects who followed Gaudi along the dithyrambic Post-Modern road couldn't hope to emulate his genius: Graves' idea of a 'decorated shed' was interesting at the time he put it forward but the buildings it inspired were shallow and pastiche-ridden; Jencks' strange four-seasons house is bewildering rather than satisfying and his glossy books make interesting reading but leave the reader curiously unconvinced. At a recent international conference in Poland delegates tried – and failed – to define what was meant by 'the Post-Modern movement in architecture'. It was indeed, they thought, a fashion and not a movement; like all fashions, its days are numbered.

### CLASSICAL REVIVAL

Classical revivalism will, I suppose, go on for ever. A few British architects ignored the precepts of the Athens Charter, rejected the teaching of the Bauhaus and the example of Le Corbusier and went on designing in a neo-Classical manner all through this century. Today an increasing number of our architects are studying Palladio and Brunelleschi – and Wren and Inigo Jones.

The development of Canary Wharf and the proposed redevelopment of Spitalfields have given our neo-Classicists an opportunity to apply their ideas. The layouts of both sites have a strong Beaux-Arts look to them, with long straight avenues, circular and crescent-shaped public spaces and a rather rigid formality very different from the mediaeval street pattern which Londoners know so well.

There seems little doubt that the neo-Classical attitude to urban design will continue and be expressed in different ways. It is to be hoped that the rigid formality and inflexibility of the Beaux-Arts tradition can be interpreted satisfactorily to incorporate the unforeseen future needs of British citizens.

179

## MODIFIED MODERN

You will have noticed that, of the ten directions in which I believe British architecture is moving today, the one which I have labelled Modified Modern illustrates a large number of buildings and projects. This has come about in answer to the severe criticism by the public of the design of many modern buildings. Here architects are confirming their belief in the precepts of the Athens Charter – to clear the slums, let the sun into every room in the house, put a green belt round every city and introduce a new era of air and light and green space. These precepts and principles make such good sense they are readily accepted by each new generation of architects. The mistakes we made in the 1950s and 1960s have now been acknowledged – and regretted;

and the part played by Post-Modernism has helped to improve our image with the public.

These are the reasons why I think the future will see the reapplication of these old principles and the arrival of an architecture with a more human face. There are already unmistakeable signs of a new spirit stalking the land and of young architects doing exciting things. There is also a new interest in architecture and the design of buildings among the media and the public, brought about principally by the Prince of Wales' interest in architecture.

All this is healthy and augurs well for the future of architecture. Modified Modern is surely the way forward.

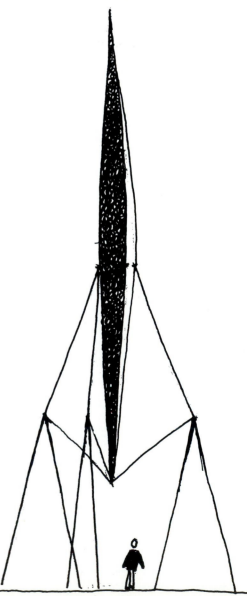

## POLITICS AND PROCESS

Some of my colleagues tell me that, in writing about architecture, it is unwise to mention politics. But sometimes I believe it cannot be avoided. If we think of architecture as the background to people's lives politics assert themselves. The decision to build the Festival of Britain in 1951 (which had a strong influence on the development of architecture in our time and was loved by the public) was a political decision; the Greater London Council (GLC) was created by a group of politicians – and abolished by another group.

Many of us think that the GLC did some splendid things while it was alive and that its abolition was a tragedy for British architecture and for London. It built the Royal Festival Hall and the South Bank Arts Centre, the Thames flood barrier, and many of our finest schools and housing estates, fire stations and public libraries; it jealously guarded London's historic buildings heritage, preventing the demolition of many fine buildings and restoring many others to their former glory; it was for many years one of the world's most enlightened regional planning authorities. (The Roehampton housing estate, overlooking London's Richmond Park, and the new town of Thamesmead are good examples of its work.)

Most important of all, however – in the context of the future of architecture and architects – the GLC was an enlightened client. With its own very large architects' department it nonetheless commissioned young architects in private practice to design some of London's important buildings. This was an imaginative policy which resulted in fine architecture and in the evolution of a happy positive relationship between the public and the private sectors. Could this be a pointer to the future? Perhaps it should.

As large national and international business organizations become larger and more powerful, as modern technology develops, as more and more public-service organizations are privatized, the need for some kind of successful collaboration between salaried architects and those in private practice becomes more and more important, and the need for a creative imaginative approach to the design of buildings, allied to a strong social conscience, is more and more evident.

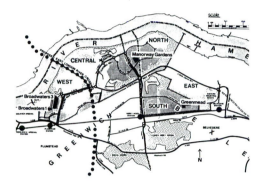

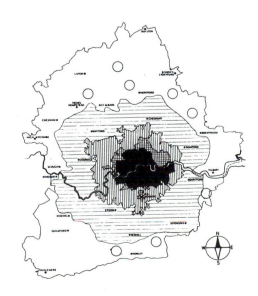

'Looking back to our past...but not copying it.' Clore Gallery, London.

Michael Hopkins' Mound stand at Lord's cricket ground

It is perhaps a strange paradox that the GLC — abolished by the Government a few years ago — showed how all this could be done — and pointed to the future.

Alone among the world's great capital cities London today has no strategic planning authority. It badly needs one and it is hoped that the current efforts of the RIBA and the RTPI to press for its establishment are successful.

All through the 1980s and 1990s many architects have been over-concerned with the elevational elaboration of their buildings. This has led to our era being thought of as 'a battle of the styles', which has meant that buildings are often considered as belonging to one category or another based on style.

And so, as the new century approaches, the so-called battle of the styles continues here in Britain and shows no sign of abating. Fortunately, however, a few of the best of our buildings manage to express the hectic eclectic age in which we live by looking back to our past and learning from it — but not copying it.

Stylistically speaking architecture in Britain today is in turmoil, echoing no doubt a society somewhat in turmoil; but this is on the whole a positive constructive turmoil, out of which may come interesting and worthwhile things.

Back in the 1970s, with his Sydney Opera House, Jorn Utzon showed how some of Australia's complex planning problems could be solved by fine architecture; in the 1990s Michael Hopkins (with his Mound stand at Lord's cricket ground) and Ralph Erskine (at Hammersmith) have done the same thing for Britain.

Perhaps — during the first few years of the 21st century — we will see some fine buildings going up at King's Cross and in London's Royal Docks area?

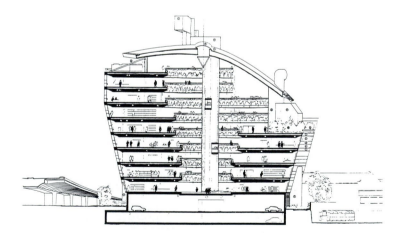

Ralph Erskine's office building at Hammersmith, London

# EPILOGUE

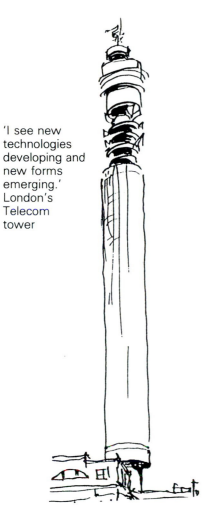

'I see new technologies developing and new forms emerging.' London's Telecom tower

I suppose crystal gazing is always a bit dangerous, but it is an intriguing exercise and may perhaps also be helpful. When I gaze into my crystal ball, with a tiny bit of my in-bred architect's arrogance still there, I see the current eclecticism continuing and (with tears in my eyes) the so-called 'international style' becoming ever-more international; I see (with bigger tears in my eyes) more giant characterless shopping malls and theme parks; I see a multi-directional push, prompted by concern about pollution and a growing interest in energy conservation and the quality of the environment; I see new forms emerging and new technologies developing – and the flexible harnessing of high technology to serve future unforeseen needs and demands; I see a stronger determination to preserve our architectural heritage and to protect our towns and cities from insensitive development, with academia and business coming closer together; and a greater patronage of the arts and architecture on the part of wealthy business organizations (good architecture equals good business); I see closer collaboration – at the design stage – between the architect and the people who will occupy his or her building; I see a continuing interest in architecture on the part of the public and the media; and I see a humbler profession, with fewer prima donnas, learning quietly and perhaps in new ways to give three-dimensional expression to the wishes, hopes and expectations of ordinary people everywhere.

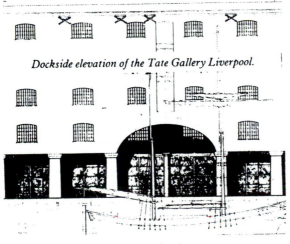

*Dockside elevation of the Tate Gallery Liverpool.*

'. . . a stronger determination to preserve our architectural heritage.'

' . . . and to protect our towns and cities from insensitive development.'

# ACKNOWLEDGEMENTS

Special acknowledgement to:
Monica PIDGEON for her wise advice and general guidance.
Dennis SHARP for his perceptive and thoughtful foreword.
Nick CLARKE (Senior Editor of my publishers Chapman & Hall) for his encouragement and tireless editorial work.

Copyright photographs are reproduced with the permission of the photographers, and drawings from journals with the permission of the editors. All other illustrations were provided by the architects concerned.

# INDEX

**Other titles from E & F N Spon**

**Architecture and Construction in Steel**
Edited by A. Blanc, M. McEvoy and R. Plank

**Auditorium Acoustics and Architectural Design**
M. Barron

**Beazley's Design and Detail of the Space between Buildings**
A. and A. Pinder

**Caring for our Built Heritage**
T. Haskell

**Design in Architecture**
**Architecture and the human sciences**
Geoffrey Broadbent

**Design Strategies in Architecture**
**An approach to the analysis of form**
Geoffrey H. Baker

**Elements of Architecture**
**From form to place**
Pierre von Meiss

**Emerging Concepts in Urban Space Design**
Geoffrey Broadbent

**The Garden City**
**Past, present and future**
S. Ward

**A Global Strategy for Housing in the Third Millennium**
Edited by W. A. Allen, R. G. Courtney, E. Happold and A. M. Wood

**The Idea of Building**
Steven Groak

**Le Corbusier**
**An analysis of form**
Geoffrey H. Baker

**Principles of Design in Architecture**
K. W. Smithies

**Shopping Centre Design**
N. Keith Scott

**The Way We Build Now**
**Form, scale and technique**
Andrew Orton

For information on these and other books, contact:
The Promotion Department,
E & FN Spon, 2–6 Boundary Row, London SE1 8HN, Tel: 071–522 9966